Child with Christ, by Bo Bartlett

THE LEARNING OF LOVE

A Journey Toward Servant Leadership

WILLIAM B. TURNER

SMYTH&HELWYS
PUBLISHING, INCORPORATED · MACON, GEORGIA
WWW.HELWYS.COM

Smyth & Helwys Publishing, Inc.
6316 Peake Road
Macon, Georgia 31210-3960
1-800-747-3016
©2000 by Smyth & Helwys Publishing

Library of Congress Cataloging-in-Publication Data

Turner, William B., 1922-
     The learning of love : a journey toward servant leadership /
     William B. Turner.
        p. cm.
     ISBN 1-573132-311-0 (alk. paper)
          1. Leadership–Religious aspects–Christianity–Fiction.
          2. Turner, William B., 1922- 3. Christian biography–United
          States. 4. Leadership–Religious aspects–Christianity.
          5. Business–Religious aspects–Christianity. I. Title.
     BR1725.T79 A3 2000
     287'.6'092–dc21
        [B]   99-045014

CONTENTS

To Sue Marie with love

Sue Marie and Bill Turner love to spend time together at their
North Carolina cottage.

Foreword

I have just finished reading the draft of Bill Turner's book. I read it in one sitting! I could not put it down. It was riveting and totally captivating. Do you want a magnificent insight into the real meaning of life? Do you want to hear from a man who truly walks the walk? Do you want a life-changing experience? Then Bill's book is for you.

I have worked alongside Bill Turner since June 1970, when his father, D. Abbott Turner, chairman of Columbus Bank and Trust Company (CB&T), asked me to serve as president of the bank. Part of my reason for considering giving up the practice of law to become a banker was the tremendous respect I had for the Turner family and their people-oriented management of the W. C. Bradley Company and CB&T.

The partnership between these great companies has grown and flourished. Today, that one $100 million community bank has grown into an $11 billion multifinancial services company: Synovus Financial Corporation, including 38 banks in four states; Total System Services Incorporated, one of the world's largest credit card processing companies; Synovus Trust Company; Synovus Securities Incorporated; and Synovus Mortgage Corporation.

The seeds sown more than 114 years ago have been the foundation for the tremendous growth of the W. C. Bradley Company and Synovus Financial Corporation. The emphasis on people development and community service has been the cornerstone for a culture that led Synovus Financial Corporation to be recognized this year by *Fortune* magazine as number one on its list of "Great Places to Work in America."

I've always known how fortunate I have been to be Bill Turner's associate, but in reading his book, I understand him better than ever before. It gave me a deep revelation of who he is and why his life has been such a great example to me and so many others.

I have said over the years that Bill Turner is ultimately the most fair man I have ever known. His book is a great revelation of the man, of the passion of a servant leader, and of a life that mirrors the Scriptures.

I intend to read it again and again. I want to give copies to my children and grandchildren. Thank you, Bill Turner, for your witness and living example of passion, common sense, and humility.

—James H. Blanchard
Chairman
Synovus Financial Corporation

In 1999 Total System Services, a division of Synovus Financial Corporation, moved into its new $100,000,000, 46-acre corporate headquarters campus on the banks of the Chattahoochee River. (Photo by Jim Cawthorne – Camera One)

Why would young people go to a senior citizen for advice and counsel that often leads to life-changing decisions? Miraculously, this has been occurring in Bill Turner's ministry with youth where for more than 50 years he has been teaching the senior high Sunday School class at St. Luke United Methodist Church in Columbus, Georgia. Succeeding generations of young people have found in Bill openness, authenticity, genuineness, absence of phoniness, and unconditional love. This half-century of transforming ministry reveals that there is no limit to how God can use a person who is willing to be vulnerable, trusting, and accepting of God's grace revealed in Jesus Christ. You cannot fool senior high youth for more than 50 years! They have discovered that Bill Turner is "the real thing."

I was Bill Turner's pastor for eight years. During that time I observed that what was happening in his ministry with youth was being played out in many other dimensions of his life including family, business, community, and philanthropy.

In this personal, vulnerable, and honest account of his own human journey he has described what happens when Christ grabs full-hold on a man—of his mind, heart, and yes, even of his checkbook. There is a Christ-centered spiritual dimension to such a life, a dimension that combines leadership and servanthood.

Jesus is quite clear that wealth can get in the way of Kingdom life. Do you remember our Lord's word that it is easier for a camel to go through the eye of a needle than for a rich man to enter the kingdom (Matt 19:24)? Jesus is straightforward: "A person's life does not consist of the abundance of possessions" (Luke 12:15).

I guess that is why I so appreciate the life and ministry of Bill Turner. Worldly resources have not blocked his vision of our Lord's will. In his story I can hear an echo of our Lord's story. "Master, you have handed over to me five talents; see I have made five more talents." His master said to him, "Well done, good and faithful servant; you have been trustworthy in these things, so I shall put you in charge of many things. Enter into the joy of your master" (Matt 25:20-21). I have observed Bill to be a faithful steward of what the Lord gave him.

The measure of a football player is not how often the ball is put into his hands; it's what he does with the ball after he gets it. Bill Turner has had a lot put into his hands and through God's grace, he has discovered what to do with it. He has carried the ball well.

Recently I heard an account of a Vacation Bible School class. All week the teacher had been teaching about the church—how the church is really people, not the building. Each session with the children ended the same way: teacher and children doing the simple finger play, each interlocking their two hands and saying: "Here is the church. Here is the steeple. Open the door, and here are the people." It reinforced the idea that the church is people. On the last day of the Bible School a new boy joined the class. The teacher did not know him, but noticed immediately that he had only one arm. She worried how the children might treat him, even make fun of him, but the class went beautifully, and the new lad fit in well. It came time for the closing. "Let's close as we have all week," she said, and as the children began to fold their hands together to form the church, the teacher was suddenly struck by the thought, "The new boy is going to be left out. He cannot clasp two hands together." Being too late to stop the class from starting to say, "Here is the church. Here is the steeple . . .," the teacher looked out of the corner of her eye and saw a young girl reaching to clasp the fingers of the newcomer's single arm. The child said to her new friend, "Let's make a church together."

Those who are servant leaders in the church, community, and the world do that. They reach out and offer what has to be done to help those around them, to include those who are excluded, to make a church and community together. Servant leadership leads by being there for others. It is a spiritual principle that has guided the Church of Jesus Christ when the church has most faithfully been the body of the servant Lord. Jesus has been called "God's Man for Others." That is servant leadership. When the church reflects the mind of the Master, the church serves. When the church lives out the will of our Lord, the church looks beyond self to the world. When the church is fully the church, there is a splendid rhythm of inviting, equipping, and serving.

Servant leaders make tough decisions. On the other hand, it is easy to make decisions when you have only yourself to please. Servant leaders make decisions that reach out to human need. Like the Dead Sea, which has no outlet, the human life that does not reach out becomes void and valueless.

Servant leaders know the worth of the gift of freedom. Servant leaders know the power of leading by example. Servant leaders know that the fullness of life is measured not by how much one has, but by how completely one gives.

This is the story of a man, a family, and their business and philanthropic enterprises, all of which have been motivated by the New Testament principle of servant leadership. While this story is a very beautiful sharing of one man's spiritual journey from birth to older adulthood, it is much more. It traces the story of a family from the 19th century to the end of the 20th century. It tells of how business and personal values instilled in one generation are passed to succeeding generations. Behind Bill Turner's story are many other stories of family and business persons seeking to live by the servant leadership principles.

This is not a finished story, but it is a story of a work in progress. I believe it is a story that will be lived out in the 21st century by succeeding generations of both family and business that will seek to live and work by the biblical principle of servant leadership.

Thank you, Bill Turner, for the courage to be open, honest, and vulnerable in the telling of your story and your family's story. What you have done invites all of us to do the same.

—Marion Edwards
Bishop
The United Methodist Church

I've always been fascinated by unfamiliar roads. They seem to offer the promise that something really good might be waiting around the bend or over the hill. But I've seldom taken the unknown path, and I've used most of my mileage traveling the same ones, much like a mule in harness wearing ruts under my feet while sometimes straining against the bit.

When Bill Turner asked me to read his journal about his own personal journey and help him write a book, I agreed, thinking here was a chance to travel vicariously on someone else's path. Here, too, was the chance to be involved in the writing of a book, something I've never done. But this was not just a book. It was a book written with Bill Turner, a man who has quietly and unobtrusively helped shape the community and region in which he lives, a man whose family heritage gave him power, prestige, and wealth but who has earned respect on his own merits.

That Bill has been and continues to be one of Columbus, Georgia's business leaders is indisputable. Blessed with vision, unbounded creativity, and the ability to inspire others, he has helped turn the companies his grandfather founded into regional, national, and international players. The W. C. Bradley Company, of which he is the former chairman of the board, manufactures Char-Broil grills, the nation's leading outdoor grill. Columbus Bank and Trust Company, where he is the former chairman of the board, holds the lion's share of the Columbus banking market. Synovus Financial Corporation, a multibillion-dollar, multifinancial services company of which Bill is chairman of the executive committee and a director, was named by *Fortune* magazine in 1999 as the best place to work in America. He is also a director of Total System Services, a Columbus-grown company that has become one of the largest bankcard data processing companies in the world. More remarkable than the fact that these companies are successful is that they all share the values and spiritual commitment of the Bradley-Turner families.

People throughout the country and the world have indirectly felt the touch of Bill Turner's hand through his board and philanthropic involvement. He served as a director of the Coca-Cola Company from 1979 to 1996, following a path blazed by his grandfather, W. C. Bradley, who was Coca-Cola's first chairman of the board, and his father, D. Abbott Turner. Concerned with the quality of education in the state, Bill served as a regent of the University System of Georgia for nine years, and is currently a trustee of Brookstone School and a trustee emeritus of Emory University.

But it is in Columbus where his influence is felt most keenly. Bill believes that to whom much is given much is expected. He has used the Bradley-Turner Foundation, where he served as chairman of the board of trustees for 35 years and is now treasurer, to satisfy his need to give back. The family's generous support has benefited educational and religious institutions, hospitals, historic preservation, not-for-profits aiding the disenfranchised and hurting, and the arts and cultural community. Bill's passion, though, has been focused on mental health since the 1950s when he helped introduce the concept of pastoral counseling to the Columbus community through the creation of the Bradley Center and later the Pastoral Institute. As a result, multitudes of people have received counseling to help them cope with the challenges life presents.

In this book Bill lovingly crafts his story of how family and faith worked together in his life to shape him as a husband, father, employer, churchman, and citizen as he searched for meaning in his life, and of how his growth led him to embrace the concept of servant leadership. Building on the foundation of caring laid by his grandfather and father and following the example set by Jesus, Bill has given words and wings to the scripture "The greatest among you shall be the servant of all." Throughout the book his stories and reflections on life shed light on the path he has taken, a journey that has touched the lives of thousands of people in his church, at the companies, and in the community.

When Bill and I first started working on this project, I asked myself, "Is Bill Turner who he purports to be? Can anybody with his power and affluence be as humble and loving as he seems, or is this just a song and dance?" (I am, after all, a journalist at heart, and we tend to be a bit skeptical.) What I discovered was delightfully refreshing. I found a man who lives his faith daily, who really does act out of love and genuine concern for others, and who is an incredibly sensitive reader of people and an equally good listener.

I also found that Bill, like all of us, has his warts—an ego that sometimes gets the best of him and an impatience when things aren't moving as fast as he thinks they should. Both are conditions of which he is aware and that he struggles to control. I think God doesn't make us perfect for a couple of reasons: We would never know His unconditional love, a love that transcends all our flaws. And we make better witnesses when others see us struggle with and master our shortcomings.

As we worked on this project, Bill and I have struggled on the incline and laughed on the downhill slope. At times we've stumbled, only to get up and try again. Through it all we have been enriched. The writing of the book made us fellow travelers on this unfamiliar road; our hearts made us friends.

—Delane Chappell

This is the true job of life, the being used up for a purpose recognized as a mighty one; being a force of nature instead of a feverish, selfish little clod of ailments and grievances, complaining that the world will not devote itself to making you happy. I am of the opinion that my life belongs to the community, and as long as I live, it is my privilege to do for it whatever I can. I want to be thoroughly used up when I die, for the harder I work, the more I live. Life is no brief candle to me. It is a sort of splendid torch which I have got hold of for a moment, and I want to make it burn as bright as possible before handing it on to future generations.[1]
—George Bernard Shaw

At the time I accepted Christ, and more importantly, accepted the fact that I am accepted, I believed that God was revealing to me new thoughts that I should pass on to "the unenlightened." I also felt that God was lucky to have someone like me on His team. Now I know better. I know that this was an exercise in ego. I have learned, slowly and sometimes painfully, that there are no new thoughts, but discovery of truth is always new. As John put it in the start of his Gospel: "In the beginning was the word," or as J. B. Phillips translates it, "In the beginning God expressed Himself." The Greek for "word" is *logos*, which is translated "the whole realm of thought." Each of us must discover for ourselves again and again this truth as we move toward ultimate truth.

I've begun to look at my journey through life as a small part of a large tapestry. My grandfather and father laid a firm foundation on which I have been able to build, and I pray that I have added to and strengthened the tapestry for future generations. Much of my contribution has been to plant and nurture the seeds of servant leadership in my family's companies and in our community. I believe that servant leadership, which is based on spirit-filled love, is the hope of the future because it leads to God. The concept has taken root in our companies as evidenced by Synovus Financial Corporation's being named the "Best Place To Work in America" by *Fortune* magazine. But even more important than the accolades we've received is the evidence I see around me day after day of people caring about one another and of people's creativity being unleashed as they explore who they are and what they can do. I see this same attitude growing in our community. It is immensely exciting.

Archimedes said, "Give me a lever long enough and a firm place to stand, and I will move the earth." I think our companies and our community can do this. We have the place to stand and the foundation that has been created for us; the only lever we need is the love of Jesus.

In this book I want to share with you my journey and how I reached this point in my life with the hope that it will encourage you and help you on your own journey, although your journey will be different from mine. This tapestry I'm creating, with its golden threads of family, church, business, and community woven together to create its pattern, is my own. Like any unique creation, it has its irregularities and imperfections. I made the mistake of trying to emulate someone else's journey and to live up to someone else's expectations. I encourage you not to do this unless your whole heart is in it. God broke the mold when He made each of us, and His plan for each of us is unique.

My journey has not always been a steady upward one. There have been spiritually dry times, times when I felt empty and God was silent. I've had plenty of failures and missteps along the way. But every time God has picked me up, dusted me off, and sent me on my way.

This book is the result of prayer. I have often sought how to pray, for much of what I read convinces me that prayer is the key to a life of love, joy, peace, fulfillment, and power. I always became discouraged when I attempted to pray because much of the time my mind wandered or I would fall asleep while praying the Lord's Prayer. Then I'd wake at 4 AM to think about Sunday School lessons, speeches, problems, people, business and community opportunities, and church. I now believe that for quite some time I have been praying effectively without knowing it. I call it my "four o'clock stuff" or horizontal prayer. It is a very refreshing and creative time for me, much better than a sound sleep. It is a time when I am so much smarter and creative than

I normally am that I truly believe I am in touch with the Creator. I suppose you could call it prayer, but it is so renewing and fun that I can't wait to go to sleep and wake up. Sometimes I get so excited that I have to get up and put thoughts down on paper before I forget them. Some of those thoughts are contained here. But prayer is much more than thoughts. It is the source of love, peace, forgiveness, joy, fulfillment, and power. It is also, as Father Lewis Everly puts it in *Our Prayer*,[2] "a gale blowing you toward others."

I believe what the Bible says: when you accept God's gift of the Holy Spirit, He will give you the gift of love. But He will also give you gifts that will surprise you. I never dreamed I could teach or counsel teenagers or come up with creative solutions to problems, but I can, and I know that this is a pure gift from God. Someone once said that a Christian is one beggar telling another where to find bread. That's what I want to do for those who read this book.

Many people have helped form my thoughts. I wish I could give them proper credit, but I can't. I'm not an orderly person who remembers the source of what now has become a part of me, but I do give credit to The Source. How gently He has shaped and corrected me.

This book began as a journal of my "thoughts while passing through" and was intended primarily for my beautiful family whom I love so dearly, and especially for my wife, Sue Marie, who is so very much a part of my own journey. She has been my companion, best friend, and lover and has never, ever let me be anything but real with her. She has shown me the real meaning of unconditional love. God has truly blessed me with wonderful sons and daughters. My family before marriage, my own family, and my sisters' families are truly remarkable and have done much to shape my life. Through the Sunday School classes I've taught for more than 50 years God has given me thousands of young people who are also very much a part of my own journey. I am eternally grateful for the love and support of my friends, the ones I grew up with and the ones I've made during the years.

As the book progressed, my definition of family grew to include all of those who work at the W. C. Bradley Company, all the branches, affiliates, and subsidiaries of Synovus Financial Corporation, Total System Services, the Pastoral Institute, and St. Luke United Methodist

Church. Then it grew some more as I realized that my friends and my community have been a significant part of my growth and that my family extends far beyond physical boundaries and blood relations because we are all God's children. I thank all of you who have propped me up, kicked me loose, pulled me back, and loved me through. This book is my attempt to give back to you some of the love you've given me. I can see now that "in all things God works together for good with those who love Him and are called according to His purpose" (Rom 8:28).

I must acknowledge and express my gratitude to Delane Chappell for her role in all of this. She is a gifted writer who has struggled to decipher, organize, and make sense of my scribbling. She even makes the finished product sound like me. But she has done more than this. She has insisted that I write about the past. My reluctance to think about the past is partially because of the pain there, and I don't want to use the past as an excuse for not being more than I am. Satchel Paige once said, "Don't look back. Something might be gaining on you." But it's necessary to look back in order to understand what lies ahead. I am excited about the future, and I'm anxious to get there because there is an urgency to accomplish as much as I can in the time I have left. But Delane's insistence that I write about the past has made me realize the solid foundation of servant leadership my dad and grandfather laid for me and for those who follow. Kiekegaard once said, "We live life forward and understand it backwards."

You don't see the completed tapestry of your life until it's finished, but if you step back and look at the portion that's complete, you get a clearer picture of how it will look when all the threads have been woven. I'm grateful to Delane for making me step back, and I'm grateful to her for the many other ways she has contributed to this work.

Please join me in praying: *Lord, let what I think be your thoughts. Let what I say be your words. Let what I do be your deeds. When I love, let it be your love. And when others see me, let them also see you. Amen.*

—William B. Turner

Chapter 1

A Firm Foundation

Therefore since we are surrounded by such a great cloud of witnesses, let us throw off everything that hinders us and the sin that so easily entangles us, and let us run with perseverance the race marked out for us. Let us fix our eyes on Jesus, the author and perfecter of our faith.

—Hebrews 12:1-2

On my eighth birthday I received a letter from "Pa-Pa," my maternal grandfather, William Clark Bradley. It was typed on white Eagle and Phenix Mill letterhead by his secretary and enclosed with a stock certificate for eight shares of Eagle and Phenix stock. The letter, which I still have, officially made me "the anointed one." It read:

My Precious Grandson:

I wish you were able to fully appreciate our love for you, and just what an important factor you are in the lives of our entire family and how anxious we all are to have you qualify for all the wonderful things we have in mind for you in the years to come. Your failure in your future responsibilities would take a great deal of sunshine out of the lives of several people I know. You are now eight years old and I want you to commence thinking about the important things of life and endeavor in every possible way to become worthy of the great responsibilities that will be yours in years to come.

This was a pretty heavy load for an eight-year-old boy to carry and probably a much heavier load for my sisters to have to bear! My grandfather played cards nearly every night, and the immediate results of his birthday proclamation were that I wanted to whip his butt whenever I had to play cards with him to show him how smart I was and that I wanted to be sure that he never found out any of the bad things I did.

I took my grandfather seriously early on, as was evident in a short speech I made on February 5, 1935 at an event honoring him. I was 12. "I am awfully glad to have been invited here tonight," the scribbled note says, "and I have enjoyed hearing all the nice things you have said about my grandfather. I just want to say that it's the truth, and I realize, on account of being his namesake, that I have a lot to live up to."

If someone were to ask me how his letter to me influenced my life, I'd have to say the letter itself didn't have much impact, but the expectations that prompted the letter had a profound influence. There was never any doubt that Pa-Pa expected me to take over as head of the family and the companies after he was gone. And there was very little doubt that I'd do it.

W. C. Bradley (left of stove) began building his legacy here in his first office, warehousing and brokering cotton.

Someone once said that the past is the prologue to the future. I believe that. To understand something of the dynamics of our family, it's important to know something of the past and to realize that as my generation has been influenced significantly by those who passed before, so too will future generations be influenced by who and what we are today.

I have never been very good with details, especially those dealing with family history. I'd much rather think about the future. Fortunately, my mother, my sisters, and others in our companies were interested in those kinds of things and have kept such family and company records as we have.

Elizabeth Bradley Turner, the only surviving child of W. C. Bradley, carried the responsibility of his legacy throughout her life.

My mother was Elizabeth Bradley Turner, daughter of William Clark Bradley and Sarah M. Hall. She married my father, Don Abbott Turner, on October 12, 1917. Shortly before her death in 1972, she wrote a short history of our ancestors as she remembered it or remembered hearing about it. As you read from the pages of the past, you'll see that she reveals something of herself in the things she remembers and the way she expresses them. Her journal is unedited, so what you read is what she wrote and how she wrote it, mistakes and all.

> I always thought that people who delved into family history and went around cemeteries looking up the dates of ancestors long since dead were peculiar—but I've changed my mind—I've gotten that way myself!

I remember once having lunch at the same table with a person of this sort. She would eat and sleep family. A dish of butter beans sat close by, and instead of helping herself and passing it on, she didn't look up from her book on genealogy until she had eaten the last bean. She would go rummaging around in garbage cans for things to read. I can see her now poking here and there with her umbrella with the hope that some bit of history would come to light. She read everything from dime novels to the classics, and when she was not reading she was writing family histories and drawing family trees.

People in general are the most interesting things on earth, and *your own* people are the most intensely interesting to you. They are the star; as they move across the stage of life, so I will try to tell you what I can about the ones nearest and dearest to my heart.

I never knew any of my grandparents. They all died before I was born, but they always seemed very real and alive to me. My great-great grandfather on my mother's side was John Hall, and his wife was Hannah Nichols of Hartford, Conn. He was born in Hartford in 1753 and died in 1830. She was born in 1760 and died in 1817. I have their family Bible with the list of births of their big family. His son, Henry Hall (my great grandfather) was born in 1782 and died in 1860. On May 26, 1808, he was married to Sarah Ann Mendenhall, of Savannah, who was born in 1790 and died in 1856. They were a most devoted couple, and I have the ring he gave her on their wedding day—a topaz surrounded by pearls. They lived in Savannah, Ga for several years after their marriage. Her parents had made their home there for a number of years. Her father, Thomas Mendenhall, was born in 1750, in Lancaster, Pa., and died in 1808, in Savannah. His wife, Hannah Poultney, was born in 1749 and died in 1800. After the war of 1812, Henry Hall moved back to Massachusetts, as business was bad in the south at that time. His two children (a boy and a girl) were born there. The son (my grandfather) Henry Thomas Hall, was born in 1817 and died in 1866.

I have always wished I could have known this grandfather. He had so much spirit and did what he felt was right, no matter what it may have cost him. In 1834, when he was only 17 years of age, he started out on a trip to see the world, and see it he did. In the curio cabinet at my mother's home we have the things he collected on this voyage, and I marvel at his choice of lovely things. Practically every country is represented in his collection. In later years he had a line of boats of his own that ran from Columbus, Ga. to Apalachicola, Florida. We have an anchor off of one of these boats at "Tree Tops." I hope it likes it's last port of call!

My grandfather settled in Columbus, Ga., where he organized the first Fire company. He had besides his boats large cotton ware-houses, and he organized in later years the Gas Company. In 1855 he was married to Elizabeth Jane Howard, who had been born in Columbus in 1828. She died here in 1873. Her parents were T.B. Howard, born July 1798, and Sarah G.W. Thweatt, born in 1805. They were married in 1822 and had sixteen children! They died and were buried in Columbus. Ga.

When Henry T. Hall and Elizabeth Howard were married, the groom's parents sent out many lovely things from Boston to furnish their new home. We still have in our possession the pictures, some of the china, and silver, they used when they first set up housekeeping.

When the war between the states started my grandfather sided with the South. This of course grieved his parents, but then his wife was a southerner, and his heart and sympathy were in the southland. He was the sole heir to George Hall, his wealthy uncle, and this deci-sion on his part cost him a large fortune. He was disinherited. There were two children from this union—a son, Henry T. Hall, and Sarah M. Hall. Sarah was my mother. Her childhood was rather sad, I think. Her father, whom she adored, died when she was quite young, and her mother, grief-stricken and ill, wore black always after this. She too passed away while my mother was still a little girl. She was reared by her maiden aunt, Mary Howard, and by her grandmother. She had many beauxs, but in 1887 she decided to marry and settle down. She had had a gay young ladyhood and had spent much time in travel. She loved pretty clothes, and some of her best ball dresses were kept and packed away carefully. I remember seeing them as a child, when they were aired in the spring and fall and packed back in the cedar closet. One dress I admired particularly. It was a heavy ivory satin, trimmed in pearls. The skirt was very full and had insets of brocade around the bottom, outlined in yellow ribbon. The bodice was tight and pointed, and the neckline was cut to fall off the shoul-ders. She was young during the "gay nineties" and went in for big picture hats with plumes, and dresses that really were creations and not just frocks! She was married to my father, William Clark Bradley, on April 27, 1887, at the First Baptist Church, by Rev. Robert Harris. The preacher called the groom William Clark *Brown* twice during the ceremony. So fearing this error would make the marriage illegal, my father corrected him the third and last time. Maybe it was too early in the morning for the minister to have collected his wits! Their wedding trip was to Niagara. It was the vogue then to honeymoon there. They had two children, a son—Forbes Bradley, who was born in February of 1889. He only lived ten days. I was the daughter, Elizabeth, and was born October 1, 1897.

The parents and grandparents of William Clark Bradley are all listed in the history of the Bradley family, but I will list the names of his grandparents on both sides very briefly below:

He (William Clark Bradley) was the son of Forbes Bradley and Theresa Ann Clark. Forbes was originally from Southington, Conn., and was born there on Dec. 1, 1809 and died in Columbus, Ga. Sept. 21, 1890. Theresa Ann was born in Columbus on April 7, 1827 and died in Russell County, Ala., Oct. 3, 1871. His grandparents on his father's side were Dan Bradley and Amy Forbes. Dan was born in 1824. On his mother's side his grandparents were William Clark and Rebecca Peddy, of Columbus, Ga. Grandfather Clark was said to have furnished the lumber off his plantation to build the first house in Columbus. He was a farmer and a Methodist preacher. Most of the Bradleys were Presbyterian. My mother, Sarah Hall, was a Baptist, as were some of the Howards. Others of this family joined the Methodist church.

My mother was sick most of her married life. She was not bitter about her lot, but went from place to place in search of health. Her chief hobby was antiques. She adored them and got much pleasure finding them in out-of-the-way places and adding them to her collection—and to mine. Her interest was also in the Kings' Daughters, which she started here. This circle was named for her, and they established the Old Ladies Home. Her love and sympathy were with this home until her death on Dec. 30, 1936.

William Clark Bradley, my father, born June 28, 1863, in Russell County, Alabama, is a big man in both body and spirit. He is a rare person—the sort that you meet once in a life time. His devotion to his family is a thing of beauty. "I can't talk about my own people," he

6

once said, "they are too close to my heart." Sometimes I think this heart of his is the biggest thing about him. His checkbook shows his generosity. Once I asked him about giving money to about four different denominations at one time, to which he laughingly replied—"Well, it will take all of the churches pulling for me to get me by St. Peter." We know better than that, but it shows how lightly he regards all of the good things he does for others. He has gone far in the business world, and his ability to see ahead and to decide some future policy is really uncanny. Big business has wanted him many times. Once I remember he turned down a job in New York that carried with it a salary larger than that of the President of the United States. He said he couldn't take all of his family up there with him and he just couldn't stand the separation. I have heard important business men say to him on several occasions—"If you say you will do it, Mr. Bradley, we know you will" so his word is his bond and he is naturally very proud of his good name and his credit.

One of the stories that has been told for many years in our company is about a W. C. Bradley Company salesman, L. A. Blau, who was in a small rural store in West Alabama. The proprietor opened the cash register, stuffed all the money into a paper bag, handed the bag to the salesman, and asked him if he would take it to the bank in Columbus for him. Astounded, the young salesman said to the man, "You've just handed me a bag of money. You don't know me. You didn't count it, so you don't know how much money is in here. What makes you think you can trust me?" The man looked him straight in the eye and said, "Son, you work for W. C. Bradley, and that's good enough for me."

In reflecting on this through the years, I realized that integrity is the greatest competitive weapon a business has. It has always allowed our companies to move ahead on a handshake rather than having to wait until attorneys get all of the I's dotted and the T's crossed. Integrity is more than honesty. It is the wholeness that allows people working together to trust each other with their lives and futures. It is a sacred trust to all who commit to servant leadership. This was the legacy our ancestors left to us.

In another accounting of our family, my mother wrote of my great grandfather, Forbes Bradley:

He was not the first of his family to come South, he was following in the foot-steps of his brothers, Henry and Edmond. The South then was a land of adventure; travel was by stage coach and frequently new roads had to be cut in the wilderness to get around a fallen tree. It took brave men to strike out and make their fortune in this undeveloped country, and I feel that Forbes must have had the same spirit as Isaac (Bradley) that carried him as a youngster from England to America (between 1660-75). Both trips were full of danger, the Sea was untamed for Isaac, and the land was full of uncivilized indians for Forbes.

He went first to Milledgeville, the capital of Georgia, and later to Columbus. This town, founded in 1828, was just four years old when he and his brother Edmond arrived. They had inherited only nine hundred dollars each from their father, and had both made small amounts for themselves in the Southland. The old saying that "what is one man's loss is another man's gain" proved true in their case. When they arrived in Columbus they went around to pay their respects and call on Mr. Powers, an old friend of the family. He was dying of cancer and made them such a wonderful offer that they took his business over. They paid him what cash they had, and he took their notes for the rest, and they stepped into one of the finest general mercantile businesses for miles around. The first year they cleared $40,000.00. Edmond stayed in the store, and Forbes sold goods out of a covered wagon to the Indians. He spoke their language as well as his own, and they always remained his friends.

Later Edmond and Forbes made a trip back to Southington (Conn) for Edmond to be married. However, true love does not always run smoothly, and the nuptials did not take place. We never knew what happened. He was a bachelor to the end, getting more peculiar and less desirable as the years passed.

Determined to bring a bride back, Forbes asked an old sweetheart to return to Dixie as his wife, and when she replied, "Well, if I could be sure you would always give me the things to which I have been accustomed, I would go South with you", he replied, "Well, I guess any damn fool would do that." He jammed his hat on his head and never returned.

Forbes married Theresa Ann Clark of Columbus, and the couple lived on a plantation in Oswichee, in Russell County, Alabama, where they raised a family of ten—Emma, Alice, Edmond, Forbes, Harriet, Mary, Dan, Fannie, William (my grandfather), and Theresa. My mother wrote:

> As a small child, I loved to hear about life on the old plantation, about "Uncle Nathan," who my father said was the original "Uncle Remus." He would tell them stories in his cabin after supper, then bring them back to the Big House wide eyed and scared to death at the tales he told. There was hunting and fishing and much farming to do, for to run a plantation in those days was a business.
>
> My father made his first money there. Grandpa paid him five cents each for doves and ten cents for quail, and he would get them by fair means or foul. Sometimes he would catch them in traps, and then again he would put corn in ditches, and when the birds would flock there, to eat, he would shoot straight down the ditch, and "Great would be the fall thereof."
>
> Once Grandpa wrote to Connecticut for a governess, and Harriett Beecher was recommended. He was slow in writing her to come, and when he did, she had gone to St. Marks, a terrible little fishing port in Florida, where some of the roughest sort of people lived. I often wonder what the outcome of things would have been had she gone to Russell County instead. Somehow I do not believe her "Uncle Tom's Cabin" would ever have been written.
>
> Grandpa would rather make ten dollars in a horse trade than in any other way, and this story illustrates the point I think very well. To begin with, many strangers stopped at the Big House, as they traveled back and forth from Columbus to Eufaula, and it was a rule never to turn a single person away. If he was just a tramp with a pack on his back he was welcomed, and if he came driving up with a prancing steed he was more than welcomed. Grandpa felt his Connecticut Yankee blood tingle in his veins, and he sensed a horse trade in the air.
>
> This day the stranger had a beautiful bay mare. Grandpa wanted her very badly. In the stable he had a handsome gray horse, but he kicked! Well, he would try to show him off. Anyway, he hoped luck would be with him. "Is the horse sound?" asked the stranger. "Sound

as a dollar" replied Grandpa. From behind a tree came a small voice—"But that horse kicks" it said. It was Dan. He liked to hang around the barn and watch the horse trades. The stranger picked up the horse's hoof. "I've done warned you" came the wee small voice. Grandpa talked faster and louder, scanning the landscape for the young culprit. The gentleman touched the horse's flank. "All right" sang out Dan, "You're going to pick yourself up in the next county." This was too much for grandpa. He had spotted his son by now, and he walked over very fast and tapped Dan none too gently on the head with his closed pocket knife. Holding his head Dan went scampering to the house. Either the stranger was deaf, or also he believed "Children should be seen and not heard", for that night the new mare was in the stable.

When the war between the states came Grandpa did not go. In the first place, he was too old, and then again, he couldn't fight against the North. But I like to hear about how he fed the Confederates, and how when the war was over great troops of them slept in the grove in front of his house. There were big camp fires and his smoke house was almost emptied of shoulders and hams. Many a broken soldier went back to his home on one of Grandpa's mules. When the regiment from Texas camped, the fences were laid low so they could ride across them as they followed the sunset trail through his fields to the West.

I like to remember, too, about Grandma, how she rode alone on the back seat of her carriage when the family went to church. It wasn't because she wasn't friendly with Grandpa, but because hoop skirts were in style, and there simply wasn't room for him to sit beside her. One day she said, "Will ought to be a fine boy, I've whipped him more than the other nine put together." I think she was right; we have lived to see her prophecy fulfilled. Most of the whippings were for going in the creek with the little Negroes on the plantation. He, or they, could not swim, and it was a daily occurrence to pull one or more of them exhausted from the water.

This same Will says that he always stood either at the top or next to the top of the class. I marveled at this, but he hastened to explain that there were only two in his class; he and Ed Patterson. Spelling was not one of his long suits, and as long as the teacher called the words out in the order they were given in the little blueback speller, all was well. But, if she skipped, all was lost. One day she did skip and the word was "hen." "A-S-S, hen" The old teacher remembered this incident all her life, and frequently she would drop by the Bank to see him, and each time she would say, "Will, spell hen", and he would always spell it, "A-S-S, hen" for her.

I'm sure that all of you know the Bradley Crest or Coat-of-Arms, with its motto, "Liber ac Sapiens Esto", and also the meaning of our name. But, in case you do not, I'll give it here; Bradley is one of the earliest surnames, being pure Anglo-Saxon, and is compounded of "Brad" which means broad, or wide and "Ley", which means a field, or pasture. Maybe that explains their love for farms or plantations. Forbes Bradley's sons all lived on big tracts of land at one time or another in their lives. And so today, I give you what information I have about the Bradleys, with the feeling that "A good name is rather to be chosen than great riches", and with the challenge, that it's up to us to keep it so.

My grandfather, W. C. Bradley, had an entrepreneurial spirit. At age 16 he left his family to attend what is now Auburn University. When his daddy died a year later, he returned home to run the plantation. I don't know why, but that didn't last long.

In 1885 he became a clerk with a cotton factoring company in Columbus called Bussey and Goldsmith. He and his brother-in-law, Sam Carter, bought Bussey and Goldsmith two years later, renaming it Carter and Bradley and adding the manufacture of fertilizer and a wholesale grocery department to its product mix. When Sam Carter moved to Atlanta in 1895, my grandfather bought out his share of the business and in 1897 incorporated it as the W. C. Bradley Company.

By 1900 he had bought the Eagle and Phenix Mills and built the largest cotton warehouse in the South. The Eagle and Phenix, which dates back to 1898, was formerly called the Eagle and Phenix Manufacturing Company.

With his businesses prospering, my grandfather Bradley turned his attention in another direction in 1888. He and his friend, G. Gunby Jordan, founded two banks: Third National Bank and Columbus Savings Bank. The banks merged in 1930 to become Columbus Bank and Trust Company.

In the late 1800s my grandfather also bought the Merchant and Planters Steamboat Line to ship groceries and fertilizer down the 365 miles of navigable Chattahoochee River from Columbus to Apalachicola, Florida, and to haul cotton back to the cotton warehouses on the return trip. He had three boats—the *W. C. Bradley*, the *Three States*, and the *Eufaula*—and would often carry passengers down the river, charging $11 for the roundtrip. In 1917 my father started working for my granddaddy on the boats. In 1980, in an interview with Susan Wiggins, W. C. Bradley Company Vice-President of Stakeholders, my father said: "One of these wags around here said that I asked Mr. Bradley if I could marry his daughter, and he told me he would let me if I would run the steamboats. That is where I got my college education—down there on the river."

At my father's suggestion my grandfather gave the boats to the Columbus Chamber of Commerce, but my dad said the cable that held them to the dock broke during some bad weather, and they went down the river and hit sandbars and sank.

My father used to say that my grandfather Bradley would buy anything if he could borrow the money, so he wasn't particularly surprised when my grandfather bought five plantations in Stewart and Quitman counties along the Chattahoochee River on which to grow cotton, corn, wheat, peanuts, and other commodities. In the interview with Susan Wiggins, my dad said of my grandfather Bradley: "I'd get him maybe twice a year to go down with me [to the farms]. He'd just spend the day and go around to all the farms and get through with it. He liked business. He liked to fish for profits. He had a shotgun. Somebody gave him a shotgun. I don't think he ever shot it. We used to shoot clay pigeons down there, and I think he went down once and couldn't hit them. He was not a hunter."

I still have the shotguns that belonged to both my grandfathers, Turner and Bradley. My grandfather Bradley's Parker double-barreled, 12-gauge is so heavy that I'm not surprised he didn't like to shoot it.

The plantations my grandfather Bradley bought, which cover about 25,000 acres, became the basis of the Bradley farm division, though most of it has become leased and managed timber land. Although my dad and I both loved the farm, farming was not in his blood nor mine. In my lifetime the farming side of the business wasn't anything I focused on. It was managed by others. But I loved to go down there. Still do. Love to hunt. Love to fish by myself in the early morning when there's mist on the water and I can sit there and be still and see beavers, deer come down to drink, all kinds of birds. Whether I catch anything doesn't really matter.

Bill Turner often seeks personal renewal in the countryside near Omaha, Georgia, where he learned to hunt and fish with his father.

In the 1920s my grandfather bought the Hamburger Cotton Mills, founded in 1888 as Paragon Manufacturing Company, and renamed them the Bradley Manufacturing Company. We sold the Eagle and Phenix and another of his holdings, the Columbus Manufacturing Company, in the 1940s to pay the taxes on his estate after his death.

In 1925 my grandfather bought the Columbus Iron Works, a company founded in 1856. Historians say the company was owned by the Teague family and manufactured farm implements and cast iron goods prior to the War Between the States. When it was leased to the government during the war, it made boilers and steam engines for Confederate gunboats. After the war it manufactured syrup kettles, sugar mills, sawmills, and a variety of farm implements. In 1882 the Iron Works produced Stratton commercial ammonia-absorption ice machines and conducted one of the country's most successful marketing campaigns for the units. In 1925 Pa-Pa converted the Iron Works to make circulating heaters and farm implements. In 1965 the Iron Works, which was in downtown Columbus next to the Chattahoochee River, was absorbed into the W. C. Bradley Company and moved into a new foundry five miles north of Columbus where it manufactured ductile iron castings. In 1971 George W. Mathews Jr., who had worked as sales manager for the Iron Works division of the W. C. Bradley Company, and a group of investors bought the foundry and renamed it Columbus Foundries. The name was changed in 1996 to Columbus Foundry L.P., and the company is now owned by Intermet Corporation.

My grandfather was also one of the early investors in the Coca-Cola Company. I don't know why this captured his imagination or why he believed in it so strongly, but he did. The thread of history that ties the Coca-Cola Company and Columbus goes back to somewhere between 1855 and 1860 when Columbus pharmacist Dr. John S. Pemberton concocted a beverage called "French Wine Coca" to sell at his apothecary shop in the city. This beverage is believed by many in Columbus to be the forerunner of Coca-Cola. There is, however, some disagreement between Columbus and Atlanta about where Coke was created. The people in Atlanta say that the drink was first served at Jacob's Drug Store in Atlanta after Dr. Pemberton moved there. But no matter what you believe, no one can deny that Columbus has played a significant role in the history of Coke. Atlanta businessman Asa G. Candler, who bought the formula from Pemberton, made the drink popular, but it was my grandfather and his close friend Ernest Woodruff who really got it off the ground. In 1919 my grandfather and Mr. Woodruff organized an investment syndicate and purchased the Coca-Cola Company from Candler for $25 million in a deal said to be the largest financial transaction in the South prior to that time. My grandfather became chairman of the board, a position he held for 27 years until 1941, and Ernest Woodruff's son, Robert Winship Woodruff, became president of the company. When the sugar crisis following World War I almost sent Coca-Cola into bankruptcy, it was my grandfather who went to New York and borrowed $4 million in his own name to help save the company.

W. C. Bradley, chairman of the Coca-Cola Company, conducts a board meeting flanked by young proteges, Robert W. Woodruff (left) and son-in-law, D. Abbott Turner (right) (circa 1925).

My grandfather died at age 84. Pa-Pa got up on a muggy Saturday morning, July 26, 1947, and dressed to go to his office at CB&T. After a good breakfast—and Grandfather loved to eat—he commented: "It's a glorious day today. I never felt better in my life." Then he walked out on the terrace and told the caretaker, Mr. A. E. Grantham: "Those are beautiful flowers, Mr. Grantham." Then he slumped over and was helped into the house. Three minutes later he died.

My younger sister, Betty Turner Corn, remembers this about Pa-Pa: "He was rather chubby and had a wonderful lap to sit in. And he'd tell stories about when he was a little boy. He was a great storyteller. I have a million stories about him. We used to go riding in his car. He grew up in the horse-and-buggy era. I can still hear him saying 'Whoa, whoa, whoa' when he wanted to stop the car. Downtown where the Catholic church (Church of the Holy Family) is, there used to be sort of a commons, and one day he knocked the fence down. He couldn't control that animal. Worst driver in the world, but he was just a darling man."

After my grandfather's death my dad took over as chairman of the board of the W. C. Bradley Company and CB&T Bancshares, the holding company for CB&T. My dad was born Don Abbott Turner in Macon, Georgia, and was one of five children. He was named for Don

Quixote Abbott, but no one knows who he was or why my dad was named for him. His family moved to Thomasville, Georgia, when he was a child, and his father was involved in the wood products business there. He was a descendent of two Methodist ministers, both of whom had served as pastor of St. Luke United Methodist Church in Columbus. Dr. Lovick Pierce, my dad's great-great-grandfather, was known as the "Nestor of Southern Methodism," and his great-grandfather was Methodist Bishop George Foster Pierce, who was the first president of Wesleyan College in Macon, the oldest women's college in the United States and the first to give women college degrees instead of certificates. In 1848 George F. Pierce became president of Emory College, now Emory University in Atlanta.

The Turner clan has strong genes. My father was one of five sons born to Grandfather and "Grannydear" Turner. Each one was short with broad shoulders. They all loved to hunt and fish, and they would modestly declare that each of their brothers was the better shot. All five were at least partially deaf from heredity and shooting a shotgun too many times, but miraculously, they could hear most of what they wished to hear. All five boys had a weird sense of humor. Their idea of a good joke was to mail one of their brothers a dead mullet wrapped as a Christmas gift with a card saying, "Do not open until Christmas."

My dad loved to tell about the time he and his brother Jack stuffed a pair of pants, socks, and shoes and placed them under the bed of their brothers Harold and Francis, leaving just the legs sticking out. When the two sleepy boys started to get in the bed, Harold discovered the intruder and said, "Francis, we forgot something," and they lockstepped out of the room and poured down the stairs.

The brothers would greet other members of the clan with "Bushwah." Whatever else that meant, it meant that you had been beaten to the greeting, so be prepared for what else might happen. If you weren't watching closely, you might find smelly shrimp in your hubcaps or a mullet in your car trunk many days later. If asked, the wives would say that the Turner men are the most stubborn men in the universe, and it was a trait they had inherited from both parents. My grandfather Turner was probably the inventor of passive resistence, and "Grannydear" was just the opposite—feisty, bossy, gregarious, loved people.

Her idea of a good time was to park on the main street, get an ice cream cone, and talk to everyone who came by. She was in perpetual motion. She would tell my grandfather what to do, and he would smile and then do exactly what he wished—which was mostly hunting and fishing until it was too dark to see.

Every group photograph of my dad and his brothers had each one straining to be the tallest of the bunch, which would probably top out at 5'7" or 5'8".

I loved to go to Thomasville where my dad's family lived. Their home was on a shady street, just a short walk from town and the Rose Theater. Thomasville is a quiet town with streets lined with live oaks, surrounded by plantations that have the finest hunting in the world. My grandparents' home was typical of the area—a two-story box with four rooms and a bath on each floor with a hall down the middle. Each bedroom had a fireplace or potbellied stove. In the wintertime, doors to each room were closed to keep the heat in. The beds had deep, soft mattresses with lots of comforters on top, and when you got in, you almost needed help to get out. I always laid my clothes out where I could reach them from the bed because I knew it would be cold in the morning before fires were lit. I also would wait until several people had used the bathroom before I got up, to be sure the Johnny seat wouldn't be freezing when I sat down.

A sun porch on the front of the house and a kitchen and a porch on the back seemed to have been added as an afterthought. There was a beautiful orange tea olive in the backyard, and my grandmother gave each child and grandchild a rooted branch to plant at their own homes. We still have ours today. Whenever the conversation in the parlor became boring, we could always go out on the sun porch where the conversation dealt with baseball, hunting, and fishing.

My uncle Harold was my hero because he managed to fish and hunt more than anyone else. He had a reputation as a bream fisherman on Lake Iamonia. He believed that the biggest bream bed was in the deepest water, and he would locate these beds by placing his nose close to the water. He got tired of people following him and fishing in his private hole, so he bought a false nose, eyeglasses, and mustache to wear while he fished. One day a boat approached, and he could hear a voice say across the water, "Naw, that ain't him, but he's an ugly S.O.B., ain't he?"

There was also a duck camp on Lake Iamonia, a bare cabin where we went to shoot ducks. There was always a contest to see who could return to the camp first with his limit of ducks.

My father left Thomasville to take a job with Columbus Power Company, a move I never fully understood. He lived at the YMCA and was involved in many athletic activities. He played basketball on a team that he claimed could beat most college teams in the area. Their star was a legend named Tippo Peddy, who my dad claimed would have been a Michael Jordan in today's game. I played against Mr. Peddy's son while in high school. Dad was also a star pitcher in baseball and was on a gymnastics team. He picked up the nickname "Golden Boy" for allowing himself to be gilded for a gymnastic exhibition.

He married my mother, Elizabeth Bradley, on October 12, 1917 in a ceremony at my Bradley grandparents' home on Wynnton Road. Then he started working for my Grandfather Bradley whom he idolized, as did my mother.

My older sister, Sarah Louise Turner, whom we call "Weezie" was born in 1920, followed two years later by me, then by my younger sister, Elizabeth Bradley Turner—called "Betty"—in 1926. Weezie married Dr. Clarence Butler, an internist. Betty married Lovick Corn, who worked in a number of areas in our company, first as the manager of the cotton brokerage and warehouse and later as vice-president of finance and vice-chairman of the W. C. Bradley Company. Lovick was an active and vital member of our team and participated in its decision-making processes. In the 40 years we worked together at the company, I found Lovick to be a Christian businessman and a devoted husband and father. He is a true southern gentleman who conveys a presence of quiet dignity, sincerity, integrity, and gentle patience. He possesses a keen intelligence and is knowledgeable of political, social, and economic issues.

Looking back, I wish that my relationship with my sisters had been closer. It's easy to make excuses, but the fact that I had been chosen so early to lead our company and our family in the future had much to do with my relationship with them. In the first place, I'm not sure that they agreed then, or even now, with that choice by my grandfather and father. Second, my preoccupation with measuring up to this responsibility and at the same time rebelling against it probably obstructed a closer relationship. Third, the fact that all three of us were trained not to "rock the boat," not to show our true feelings, was a further hindrance. I'm sure there was some anger, jealousy, frustration, and feelings of competition as well as inadequacy on all our parts. It is impossible to connect with others if we don't show our true feelings, and I hope I've done a better job of that in recent years.

I always felt my older sister, Weezie, was superior to me in many ways, and I'm sure she thought so too. She was self-assured, all-knowing, and confident, and took the responsibility seriously of seeing that I was "raised right." Once when I was a little boy, I was lying on the floor and she got on top of me, held me down, and teased me about being too weak to get up. I'm sure that she was trying to impress me with her position of leadership, but it made me so angry that when I did get up, I threw a brass candlestick at her that knocked the glass out of our front door. Fortunately, I missed my target. My mother made me write, "A soft answer turneth away wrath" 100 times. So I learned further to give a soft answer rather than deal openly with the competitive spirit that existed between us.

After Weezie's marriage to Clarence Butler, my dad often referred to her as "General Butler" because of her ability and desire to be in charge. As an adult, Weezie's great leadership ability showed in the role she played in the development of the Historic Columbus Foundation and the Columbus Museum. These two organizations were the springboard that launched the Columbus Challenge, a community initiative that raised $86 million in the late 1990s and was the beginning of the cultural renaissance in Columbus. I will always be grateful for the way she covered up for me during my teenage years and for the support she and Clarence gave me while I was chairman of the W. C. Bradley Company and the Bradley-Turner Foundation. Sue Marie and I will always remember a wonderful trip we had years ago with Weezie and Clarence driving through Spain. Before other members of our family became interested in hunting, Clarence and I were regular hunting buddies for many years.

I wish I had been a better role model for my little sister, Betty. Betty was a cute little thing with curly hair and dimples. I'm afraid I picked on her some of the time. My friends and I would make Betty and her girlfriends put on boxing gloves and go at it while we acted as their trainers. Maybe that's why Betty grew up to be such a tough, strong, independent character. When Betty was a teenager, I felt it was my duty to protect her from the boys—and there were lots of them—who came around. I remember once my dad referring to one of her dates as a "nice teenage boy," and I remember wanting to tell him that there was no such thing as a "nice" teenage boy! She had many friends and suitors, but also loved to spend time in her room doing all kinds of creative things. As an adult, her creative gifts have blossomed in many ways, but especially in her painting, and I'm proud when I see her paintings at art exhibits. Betty has never lost her charm.

The summer I asked Sue Marie to marry me, she and I had decided to allow our relationship to cool off for two weeks. She and her family went to Atlantic Beach, and my family went to Sea Island. After two days Betty could see that I was "pining away" and encouraged me to drive to Atlantic Beach and get Sue Marie, which I did. I will always be grateful for the shove she gave me.

Thoughts While Passing Through

- Even when we don't see God, He sees us.
- If we try to love on our own, we will be crushed by the ingratitude of people. But if we love God, nothing can stop us from loving people.
- The road we travel every day is the road to Emmaus.
- The things that make me the most angry with others are the things I hate about myself.
- There is no future in living in the past.

CHAPTER 2

HOW I GOT TO WHERE I AM

"For I know the plans I have for you," declares the Lord, "plans to prosper you and not to harm you, plans to give you hope and a future. Then you will call upon me and come and pray to me, and I will listen to you. You will seek me and find me when you seek me with all your heart."
—Jeremiah 29:11-13 (Phillips)

My Grandfather and Grandmother Bradley lived on Wynn's Hill in the Wynnton neighborhood. There were two entrances to their estate. One at the foot of Wynn's Hill led to a swimming pool and a small fishing pond. The main entrance at the top of Wynn's Hill had brick pillars on either side that said to me, "Put on your good behavior. Children should be seen and not heard. Remember your manners." Their house later became the home of the Columbus Museum.

I always preferred the back entrance. The main entrance led to the house that even then reminded me of a museum on the ground floor. The second floor consisted of a parlor/loggia with two bedrooms on each end. My grandfather occupied one bedroom, and my grandmother occupied an adjoining bedroom.

When I think about this, I remember the strong smell of Absorbine Junior that came out of my grandfather's room because of the massage he received each morning. My recollection of my grandmother's room is of her being bedridden and on crutches and of her having a nurse a good bit of the time. There was a small elevator just outside her door because of her arthritic condition.

On the ground floor was a cozy den with a fireplace. This was where the grownups usually sat and where my grandfather held court. He was a great storyteller, and the adults seemed to enjoy him immensely. At least, they laughed at everything he said. The children usually stayed in a large living room that connected to the dining room, and we were expected to behave. If I cut up too much, my dad would come out and give me a pat on the head and tell me to "be nice." The result of this pat always had the desired effect. What most people didn't know was that he wore a heavy gold ring that he would turn around on his finger before he gave the pat—a loving pat that could raise a knot on my head the size of a marble. Whenever I saw him turn the ring around, I knew it was time for me to shape up.

The furniture in the living room was large with big claws on the legs. The armrests were animals with teeth poised to take a bite. All of these chairs had horsehair covers that scratched our legs. There was one place in this room that we loved, especially on Sunday nights. We would sit on a sofa—the only comfortable furniture in the room—and listen to a large radio that "could get WLW Cincinnati" where "Amos and Andy" and "Major Bowles' Amateur Hour" enthralled us. Major Bowles would present an amateur to sing, and if the singer didn't perform up to the Major's expectations, he would ring a gong, and it was all over for the performer. Many a career was nipped in the bud by the Major's gong.

Mealtimes at the "Big House" were an experience. Mostly the food was delicious, but sometimes there were things like brains and eggs, possum, and buttermilk. Some of the adults raved about these delicacies because they were my grandfather's favorites, but I couldn't swallow without gagging, so I would find an excuse to leave the table. My grandfather also loved an innocuous dish called rice pudding. The butler's name was George Hill, and he had previously been a steward on one of the riverboats. Whenever he served my grandfather rice pudding, my grandfather would say, "George, I can hear the *Queen City* coming round the bend."

After my grandfather's death in 1947, my mother and dad and the stockholders of Eagle and Phenix Mills donated my grandfather's house and the property on Wynn's Hill to the Muscogee County

School District. The Board of Education built the W. C. Bradley Memorial Library in 1950 near the lake and pool on the property and turned the house into the home of the Columbus Museum in 1953 through a gift from the William C. and Sarah H. Bradley Foundation.

Their house, sitting on a hilltop with a view almost to the Chattahoochee River, was, some said, a showplace with grounds designed by the world-renowned landscape firm of Frederick Olmstead. In recent years the Columbus Museum, with the help of the Junior League of Columbus, has restored some of the landscaping to its original state.

Today, when I go in the Columbus Museum, I still get the feeling that it's time to shape up and be nice, even though my grandfather's house blends in well with the beautiful museum.

The house that I grew up in—also on Wynnton Road—was smaller than my grandfather's house, though its grounds were also designed by the Olmstead firm and included a rose garden, vegetable garden, a sunken garden, a fan-shaped boxwood garden, three reflecting pools, and a pergola of roses. The house later became Trinity School, the forerunner of Brookstone School. It was demolished in the 1970s, and a Starvin' Marvin gas station was erected on the site.

We lived only two blocks from Wynnton Elementary School, but my mother insisted we had to be delivered there each morning in a seven-passenger, chauffeur-driven limousine. When we protested, we were told that we were different, a pronouncement that in all my years of life I have never been able to shake. As a result, I became adept at two things as a child: rolling out of the car in a way that kept most of my fellow students from seeing me and becoming handy with my fists when I was teased.

My sister, Weezie, did some writing about the "olden days" for her grandchildren, and I include some of her remembrances here because she remembers our childhood better. She said:

> In our yard, besides the things of beauty, were a dog pen for Daddy's hunting dogs, a rabbit hutch and, at one time or another, a goat, ponies that kicked and bit us and ran away, ducks, pigeons, fish, and dogs of our own. There was also a large chicken yard where one of our favorite forms of entertainment was to watch Lige wring a

chicken's neck for our dinner. Obviously, it didn't take much to amuse us. Although I do not recall our yard smelling bad with such a menagerie in residence, it certainly must have. I do remember there being a lot of flies in our yard.

To help take care of the large house and the three of us, my parents had household help. Our favorite was Sarah Speller, whom we called "Mammy." In her writings Weezie describes her as:

. . . short and fat with a wide comfortable lap on which we were cuddled, rocked, and comforted. Her skin was reddish brown, her cheekbones high, an inheritance from her Indian grandmother. Always she wore an ankle-length blue and white uniform covered by a long white bibbed apron. There was a close fitting white cap on her head and black oxfords on her feet. Mammy called me "Baby" and Bill "Brother" and the three of us were inseparable. Most of these memories are of the two of us because Mother had hired a white nurse to look after our baby sister. This infuriated Mammy who was hardly civil to the nurse, and she completely ignored Betty. It was not until Mother realized her error in judgment and turned Betty over to Mammy that she began to like her. She needed a new baby because Bill and I had started to school. Mammy spent hours curling her hair and dressing her up.

"Mammy, if I bit you would you be white on the inside like a chocolate marshmallow?" Bill asked one day. He was sitting in her lap, one hand on her cheek, looking like he was contemplating doing just that. I thought that was a pretty rude thing to say, but Mammy just smiled, patted him, and said, "Naw, Brother, I'm black through and through."

After we were a little older our favorite place to visit was Mammy's room. She was an expert wine maker, using the grapes from our scuppernong arbor. The room smelled sweet and musky, and there were huge crocks covered with cheesecloth and some sort of tubes draped overhead. Mammy would give us each a tin cup containing a small amount of wine. One day, one of us dared to say, "Mammy, we got terrible colds. Could we have one of your Dr. Blossor Mentholated cigarettes?" We all sat there and giggled and smoked and drank wine. We thought this was the most grownup, fun thing we had ever done. Nobody ever mentioned it to Mother.

One day as we were driving home from school, Ben (the chauffeur) started laughing and teasing Bill that the "Little Boss" was still a baby because his mother wouldn't let him walk to school. Bill reached out and gave Ben a karate chop on the back of his neck, and Ben slumped over unconscious. Fortunately, he was driving his usual 10 miles per hour and Bill guided the car to the curb where we waited until Ben regained consciousness. After that, Ben never mentioned this sore subject again. No one told Mother.

But most of our days were not all that exciting. Many of my memories are of sunny days spent under our Scuppernong Arbor. There was a swing and a sand box under the arbor, and close by a slide, a see-saw, a joggling board, and my doll house. There always seemed to be a breeze and we must have eaten a ton of sweet slippery scuppernongs every summer.

Every time Bill managed to find a "little pocket change," he would buy himself a knife. As soon as he purchased one, he would lose it. It was a real mystery. He could never recall how he had lost it. When he became 16, Mammy presented him with a whole collection of knives. "I reckon you's old 'nuff now to have a knife," she told him.[3]

I got in my share of scrapes growing up. Some I've been willing to confess. When I received an award from the Chattahoochee Council of Boy Scouts at an awards banquet several years ago, I felt compelled to tell this story on myself. Each year a "sacrificial lamb" is chosen to be "roasted" at a fundraising dinner and all of his/her friends must pay to come to honor the lamb. It's a good way to raise money for a worthy cause, but I was not a very worthy recipient because I had been kicked out of the Boy Scouts. Well, not exactly kicked out, but not encouraged to stay either. What happened was this: A friend and I were sitting in the back of the Scout meeting room at Wynnton School. We were cutting up, acting silly, and being disruptive, and the rest of the troop was giggling. The Scoutmaster asked us to go outside until we could behave. Well, there was a big trash can full of paper sitting outside the window and, like all good Scouts, we were prepared—with matches. We thought it would be exciting to light the paper and yell "fire!" What we weren't prepared for was the draft from the fire that caused the burning paper to float into the Scout room. If there hadn't been 20 other equally prepared Scouts and their Scoutmaster to stomp out the fire, we would have probably burned down Wynnton School. When the smoke had cleared, the Scoutmaster suggested that my friend and I might want to find other creative ways to burn off our excess energy.

Now, I have always told my children to be real and not be phony. So, on this occasion, they told me that they expected me to confess my sins at the Scout banquet, so I did. I confessed arson to show that somehow God can change the dumbest, most undisciplined person if we give Him a chance.

My fondest memories of my childhood and youth are the times I spent with my dad. When I was a little boy, I used to stand on the corner, baseball glove in hand, looking for my dad's car. On the hottest summer day he would play catch with me and show me how to throw a curve ball. Most of the time he let me tag along with him hunting and fishing. I still remember riding in the back of Mr. Albert Woolfolk's old Plymouth—no seats, no heater, but two wonderful smelling bird dogs named Frank and Queen, one under each arm to keep me warm.

I loved sitting in my daddy's lap after he had returned from hunting and picking beggar lice seeds off his sweater and pants. The smell of dogs, birds, woods, and smoke to me is still a wonderful aroma.

The meals my dad cooked in the field were wonderful. He'd take the quail we'd killed and shake them in a sack with flour and salt, then place them over the fire in a can of lard until they rose to the top. We'd eat them with light bread and gravy made from the lard. It couldn't possibly taste as good as I remember.

My dad taught me to make every shot count when I was hunting. He charged me five cents for each shell I used and paid me 10 cents for each bird I killed. Once when I was having a bad day and was about a dollar in the hole, I noticed six doves sitting on a telephone line, and I shot all of them with one shot! After repeating this several times, I was financially solvent once again. But all the telephones in that region were out of order. This put an end to our financial arrangement.

John Jackson was my hunting "nurse" who kept me out of further trouble. He called me "Little Boss" and taught me much about the outdoors. Even when I was much older, if I shot my gun, John Jackson would miraculously appear about 15 minutes later to hunt with me.

I remember how proud my dad was the first time I beat him shooting, and I have had this same bittersweet experience with my own sons and grandsons.

My dad taught me many lessons as I was growing up. One that stayed with me through the years was never to kill anything that you weren't going to eat. Usually he would let me tag along when he went hunting but for some reason one day he left me at home. The Cedar Wax Wings were flying through, and I was determined to show him I belonged in the field. I killed 50 Cedar Wax Wings with my BB gun. When my dad returned, he told me, "Clean them and get ready to eat them because you never kill just to be killing." Fortunately, we had a cook who could make a bird pie, and it wasn't so bad. My dog thought it was great!

Through the years I have collected Parker shotguns, and I have given each son and grandson one of these guns when they graduated from my school of safety, shooting, and sportsmanship. Once during the school year Bill, my oldest grandson, and I were sitting together in an early dove field—hot, dirty, gnats in our noses, eyes, and mouths—and Bill said, "You know, it doesn't get any better than this." I knew he was right, and I knew the Turner genes still ran strong.

My family used to go to Atlantic City a lot. My grandmother and mother liked to go up there for some reason. My dad and granddad would go on to New York, and we'd stay in Atlantic City on the Boardwalk. We'd ride in the wheelchairs and go to the Million Dollar Theatre to see all the shows. When we went to New York, we'd stay at the Astor Hotel, which is right on Times Square. Dad would go downtown to work, and the girls and mother would go shopping. They'd leave me alone, and I'd go to the Penny Arcade or to Stillman's Gym where the great boxers worked out. I can't believe my dad let me walk around New York like that by myself. When I got older, I started going to the burlesque shows.

My dad also took me to many baseball games at Yankee Stadium and to the Polo Grounds. I saw all of the superstars of that era—Babe Ruth, Lou Gehrig, Joe DiMaggio, Yogi Berra, Jimmy Foxx, Mel Ott,

Carl Hubbard, and others—and I had many autographed baseballs from them. Unfortunately, I used those balls in sandlot games until the names wore off. I once caught a foul line drive off the bat of Yogi Berra while sitting in a first base box. The Yankee usher made me sign an injury release, but I got to keep the ball.

One of the great experiences of life is in reversing roles with your father and becoming the one who "tries" to be the caretaker in his later years. My dad was still a handful as he grew older—stubborn, fiercely independent, not wanting anyone to tell him what to do. My sisters and I became concerned about his driving ability, and they elected me to confront Dad. I made up a story and told my dad that our company insurance might be canceled if he didn't agree to having a driver. Unfortunately, he knew the president of the company and yelled out to his secretary to "Get Joe _____ on the phone." When Joe came on, Dad said, "Joe, what's this crap about y'all canceling our insurance?" and that was the end of that, and I had to try another direction.

My dad and Ed Gates, who was the head of Williams Construction Company, went fishing every Thursday and Saturday afternoon. Both Ed and Dad would tell you that they were each going fishing for the other's health. They were like two little boys planning their outings. Between them they had eight lakes to choose from, and it would usually take six or eight phone calls, starting Monday morning and ending Thursday morning, to determine their destination.

They had lost their boat paddler who worked for Ed, so I plotted with Ed and convinced Dad that it was his turn to furnish the boat paddler. I found a wonderful man, J. C. Flagg—who was also a preacher —to be their paddler and dad's driver. Dad agreed that J. C. could be his driver if he could drive himself on Saturday and Sunday. I knew his freedom was important to him, so I agreed, but I trailed him in my car to check his driving many Saturdays and Sundays.

Dad and J. C. hit it off immediately, and I'm sure their philosophizing together helped J. C. with his Sunday sermons. Once when J. C. was driving Dad back from a Coca-Cola Company directors meeting in Atlanta, J. C. became unusually quiet. After persistent questioning from Dad, he admitted that he was a little put out because the other drivers had Mercedes and Cadillacs, and they were kidding him about driving a Ford. Dad said, "Well, J. C., what kind of car do you think we should have?" J. C. replied, "I think we should have a Mercedes." Dad said, "Well, go get us one." J. C. went down the next morning and traded for the car, and Dad bought it sight unseen. I think this indicates the kind of relationship they had, but it also indicates how much Dad prized his independence.

D. A. Turner, Ed Gates, and Rev. J. C. Flagg philosophized about the nature of God and man on their many fishing excursions.

Mrs. Gladys Locke served as secretary for my father, Lovick Corn, and me. I never saw this remarkable lady lose her temper, and she had the best telephone voice of anyone I ever heard. First impressions are lasting ones, and she played a major role in creating a great impression of what the W. C. Bradley Company was like. She loved my dad, and she was a great help in keeping us working together.

To keep Dad out of trouble during his later years, Mrs. Locke and the ladies at the bank developed an elaborate spy system to be sure we knew what Dad was doing. He was fiercely independent and didn't want me telling him what to do. Dad's habit was to spend the first two hours in the morning at his W. C. Bradley Company office and then go to an office at CB&T where he held court with whomever came in. This was a wonderful arrangement for the bank because Jimmy Blanchard, the bank's president, was out of his office a good bit of the time calling on customers and performing various kinds of community service. Dad used to give Jimmy fits about not being at his desk, and I could tell that it was getting on Jimmy's nerves because he was working very hard doing what he thought best for the bank. I suggested to Dad that he might lighten up on Jimmy, so he called Jimmy into his office and asked, "Jimmy, am I bothering you?" Of course, Jimmy replied, "Oh no, sir, Mr. Turner." Then Dad said, "Well, you know I could if I wanted to." So much for my lesson in employee relations. Fortunately, Jimmy loved Dad as much as I did and understood him just as well. My role became one of joining with Jimmy to "gang up" on Dad when we wanted to do something that was different from the old ways at CB&T.

When Ed Gates was no longer available to fish and hunt with my dad, I tried to arrange my schedule so I could be available to take him as often as possible. If I made a date to take him fishing at 1:30, I knew that he would be standing in my driveway with his rod and tackle box in hand by one o'clock. When I couldn't take him, either his grand-sons, sons-in-law, or Neal Gregory, who was secretary/treasurer of the W. C. Bradley Company, took him.

I also arranged for an easy place for him to shoot quail. He was in his mid-80s and was not as quick or as coordinated as he had once been, so we put out pen-raised birds that didn't fly as fast as wild birds for him to shoot. He never let on that he knew the difference, but I know that someone who had hunted quail for 75 years did know.

By that time, Dad was nearly stone deaf, which he handled by doing all of the talking while I drove the car. This was a wonderful opportunity for me to get a better understanding of my dad and of myself. On one of those outings he told me that he had considered himself to be a caretaker until I could take over the business. He was far, far more than that, and his values still govern my life and our companies.

Because of Dad's age, I was prepared to have to bring his body back to Columbus in the back of the station wagon after one of those outdoor excursions. Fortunately, I never did. When he had a stroke at age 89, he was still looking forward to hunting that fall. What a perfect way for him to go.

Someone once said that children are good recorders of information but poor translators. My dad always told me that he was proud of me when I did something well. I translated this to mean that my worth as a person depended on my performance. There was no room for failure in my life. He never told me he loved me until just before he died, but

I know now that his saying he was proud of me was his way of saying he loved me.

One time, coming back from fishing, my father also told me that the secret of happiness is having something to do, someone to love, and something to hope for. That was something that always stuck with me. He had all three, and so do I.

Thursdays were sacrosanct to D. A. Turner, or "Mr. D. A.," as he was fondly known. He allowed nothing to interfere with his fishing and hunting day.

My mother was a very beautiful, but very complex person. She was an only child who, I always sensed, felt guilty because her brother had died and left her with the obligation to produce the successor to my grandfather. She graduated from National Park Seminary in Washington, D.C., with a degree in dietetics, but I don't recall her ever cooking very much, and yet our food was delicious. She never spanked me, but she was a master at laying a guilt trip on me whenever I did wrong. Then she would make me read the Bible.

My mother had lots of friends, but seemed to get her feelings hurt easily. She had a knowledge of horses, but I don't remember her riding with the rest of the family often. Yet she took a very strong interest in my sister Betty's riding. She even stood up to my dad and grandfather once so that Betty could compete in a national championship. When

Betty won the Five-Gaited Pony Class in Lexington, Kentucky, on her horse Hot Shot Charlie, they were just as proud as my mother.

Betty, Weezie, and Bill Turner loved riding horses. Sometimes they would be joined by their father, who taught them a genuine love and appreciation of the outdoors.

My mother was a marvelous hostess who loved to entertain. With guests she could keep a conversation going without periods of silence, a skill at which I always marveled. She was a meticulous housekeeper, but still she allowed her children to smoke rabbit tobacco in the house and to roller skate in the back hall. She loved flowers and passed this love on to all her children. She was a master flower arranger and encouraged us to have exhibits at the county fair. We won several ribbons.

Physically, Mother was small and delicate, almost fragile in appearance, and yet she had the strength to pull three drowning children from my grandfather's pool. My sister Weezie and I were both good swimmers, and one day we dared one of her friends to jump off the diving board and promised that if she'd do it, we would support her. When she jumped, she grabbed both of us, literally in a death grip, and we sank to the bottom of the pool. I can remember the peaceful "at home" feeling I had until my mother jumped in and pulled us to safety. Mother was not a good swimmer. She swam the side stroke, but she saved our lives. Maybe the strength generated by love is why I've always felt at home at sea and know that death, when it comes, will be peaceful and like going home.

My mother was a kind, giving, and thoughtful person, but she somehow conveyed to me that you do good things out of a sense of duty rather than out of love. This is something that continues to plague me to a degree. My feeling about her was that she did things for us because that was what mamas were supposed to do. She always said, "You always do the right thing," and that's been kind of a burden for me in both my personal and business life. I started out in the company doing things because of a sense of duty. I was supposed to. That was what everybody expected of me. Tied closely to that, I think, is my need for approval. If I do what I'm supposed to do, people will approve of me.

My mother didn't come across to me as being a happy, joyous person. In fact, she seemed to have a difficult time showing her feelings. She worshiped her father, and no one could ever measure up to him—including me.

The closest I ever felt to her was just before she died. She was in the hospital for an operation and was doing pretty well. I left home one day feeling guilty because I knew I had a busy day and wasn't going to have time to get by to see her. But on an impulse, I stopped by the store and bought her some hand lotion and took it to her. When I went into the room, she began, "You didn't have to do that . . ."

Finally, I said, "Mother, I know I didn't have to, but I did it because I love you," and I sat down on her bed and took her hand. "Mother, do you remember the time I had the measles and you sat by my bed and read a Raggedy Ann story about a wonderful tree that if you asked it for something to drink, it would give it to you? Raggedy Ann asked for a strawberry milkshake. That milkshake sounded like the most wonderful thing in the world. I remember that as you finished the story, I was thinking, 'This is what mothers are supposed to do. This is their duty.' You turned out the light and left me there, and I thought about that milkshake. In a little while the light came back on, and you came into my room with a strawberry milkshake. That was the time I most felt love because it was something you didn't have to do."

I'll never forget the radiance on my mother's face as she began to tell me about her childhood and how her mother was bedridden from the time she was a little girl and how she was an only child and she was lonely and how she worshiped her father. He was a businessman and very busy, and the only way she could get his attention was to perform, paint a picture, sing a song, or do a dance. When she would do that, he would take her on his lap and talk to her about his values of honor and integrity and duty. For the first time I began to understand my mother and accept her as well as love her. We talked there for a few minutes, and God was in that room. A nurse came in and interrupted, and Mother said, "You are going to be late for your meeting; you'd better leave." As I went out the door, she called me back. I knew she was going to say, "You always do the right thing" because that is what she usually said, but instead she said, "I love you."

When I got to my meeting, I was greeted by one of the secretaries who told me, "You are to return to the hospital at once." I knew something bad had happened. I dashed back to the hospital and ran up the stairs. As I came out of the stairwell, the doctor was coming out of my mother's room, and he shook his head and said, "We couldn't save her." She had an embolism and had gone into cardiac arrest.

I leaned back against the wall with my eyes closed trying to collect my thoughts and catch my breath, and I heard one of the nurses say, "Isn't it a shame he got here too late?" I wanted to shout at her, "I was almost too late, but I wasn't too late."

Death is not the greatest tragedy in this life. It is not even in living a short life. The real tragedy is wasting one moment without experiencing God's love flowing into us and through us toward another. Through the years God has poured oceans of love into me, and that has enabled me to reach out and love as He loves. Nothing can come close to touching this experience.

Someone asked me how I would describe my life. I said that the first part was pain; the second, duty; and the third, joy. I wasn't unpopular as a teenager, but I didn't date much because I always feared rejection. I didn't want to be rejected. I'd even sit around waiting for my friends to call me and say, "Let's go do something."

As it has turned out, the insecurities I felt in my youth have been a blessing because I can identify with the teenagers who come to me for counseling. That's one of the things I have had going for me teaching teenagers in Sunday School because those things haven't changed. These teenagers feel the same way I felt.

As a teenager, my friends and I did some things that today make me shake my head in wonder. We had a group that we called the Little Theater Club. The fact that we did this proved we didn't have anything to do. We'd meet over where Dee Dee Stelzenmuller's dress shop is now at St. Elmo. It was a drugstore then. After work somebody would come up with ideas of something for us to do, four or five suggestions, and we'd vote on which one we were going to do. Then we'd flip a coin or match to see who had to do it. There was an abandoned church on Forrest Road, right after you turn off Macon Road, and everybody who wasn't performing had to get in that church and peep out the cracks at whatever the performance de jour was. One stunt I had to do was the mad dog act. We picked up two girls to ride them around. My hand was all wrapped up in a huge bandage. You couldn't miss it. They said, "What's wrong with your hand?" I said, "Well, a dog bit me. They've got him under observation, but it's nothing to worry about I don't think. They said it would take a few more days to find out if he was rabid or not."

We'd get on out there near that church and I'd start, "I'm not feeling good. I'm really not feeling good." We'd pull in there by the church. I'd put some toothpaste in my mouth, and the fellow in the back seat would do the same thing. Then I'd just go mad. He would reach over to calm me, but I'd bite him and he'd immediately go mad. Those two girls didn't even open the door of the car. They went out the window.

We had another stunt where we'd all dress up like thugs, and one of us would take a date out and park. Then the thugs would show up and start cussing, and the hero would get out of the car and say, "You can't talk like that around my girl," and immediately knock six guys out. Girls just loved that. One little girl told her brother, "That Bill Turner is the fightingest man I've ever seen." One time there was a guy playing the hero, and we double-crossed him. When he said, "You can't do that around my girl," we jumped him and rolled him down the hill. He was yelling, "Y'all aren't supposed to be doing this."

I graduated from Columbus High School and entered Georgia Tech at age 16, and for the first time I felt like I was running my own life. But I didn't do a very good job. To borrow an expression from my grandfather, "It was like throwing biddies (baby chickens) in the branch." I wasted four years at Tech and graduated by the skin of my teeth. The event prompted one of my cousins to send me a graduation present with a card that read, "I send this little gift as a token of my amazement!"

On the first day of orientation at Tech an indifferent, pompous official stood before the entire freshman class and said, "Take a look at the person on your right and left. One of you will be gone by spring." I thought that was a pretty cold, uncaring statement to make to 16- and 17-year-olds and especially so because the boys on my right and left looked eager and bright compared to me, but I made a vow that I wouldn't be among the third missing come spring. At that point my motivation became beating the system—not learning. I studied the teachers rather than the subjects, and I became a master at predicting what teachers would ask on quizzes and exams. It didn't hurt that I was able to go to the tutoring center for athletes because I went out for freshman basketball and later for swimming.

I was barely able to keep my head above water for four years, but what I really majored in was movies. I bet I averaged at least one picture show per day and two on Sundays. Our favorite day was Thursday because we didn't have afternoon classes. My friends and I would go to the Davidson-Paxon Department Store dining room for lunch. The store featured a plank steak and trimmings for two for $1.50, and they also had a fashion show. We would share the steak and ogle the models before catching the first show at Lowe's Grand Theatre. We would then catch the second show at the Paramount Theatre next door, and then retire to the Dinkler Hotel Owl Room for a beer before dinner. We always hoped that we would be able to pick up some of the working girls who frequented this watering hole, but we never did, probably because of the six- to seven-year age difference in favor of the girls. We would then adjourn to Herrens Restaurant for a Manhattan cocktail and prime rib (another special) before returning to campus. Or on a good night we might take in a third movie at the Rialto Theatre right across the street. To this day, when I see an old movie, I can name all the characters, even to the bit players. It's a shame I didn't approach my studies with the same enthusiasm. We were even watching a movie when the Japanese bombed Pearl Harbor.

I had a bit of a problem in the spring of my freshman year. My dad had me make out a budget for my entire freshman year at Tech, and then he opened a checking account for me at C&S Bank. Unfortunately, my money ran out in April with two more months of school left, and I wasn't about to ask Dad for more money. Fortunately, I had paid my fraternity bill at the beginning of the spring semester, so at least I had a good breakfast. I hadn't signed up for lunch or supper because of my movie schedule. And fortunately, a friend and fraternity brother, Bob Goree, would take me home for lunch most Sundays. But what really saved me was a carhop nicknamed Snake-Eye who worked at the Varsity Drive-In Restaurant. During my solvent days I was a lavish tipper at the Varsity. One day Snake-Eye spotted me walking by the Varsity (no gas for my car) and asked why I hadn't been in. I said, "Snake-Eye, I'm broke and can't afford to eat at the Varsity anymore." Every afternoon from then to the end of school Snake-Eye bought me a chocolate milk and a hamburger. I repaid Snake-Eye with interest when I got a summer job after school was out. I also hocked my pocketwatch and sold my books to make ends meet.

There is only one teacher at Tech that I remember with great affection. Professor Hubert Dennison was head of the industrial management department, and the story was told about him that he was a lawyer who had made and lost a fortune in the Florida boom and had dropped out of the rat race to teach at Tech. He could regale us for hours with stories about his career.

I remember one lesson in particular that he taught. He wrote in big letters on the blackboard "Responsibility and authority must coincide." Then he said, "Tomorrow I'm going to ask you to write an essay on all the reasons that statement is true." Then he left the class.

He also had us study the stock market and pick a stock to follow. He would grade us on our investment results for the semester. My two stocks were Montgomery Ward and Sears and Roebuck. In fact, their potential looked so good, I had my dad invest my summer earnings in those stocks. When I went into the Navy, I asked Dad to sell the Montgomery Ward stock and use my Navy pay to buy timber land in Harris County for me and start a selective cutting program, reinvesting the proceeds in more Harris County land. Land was cheap back then, and I now have 2,000 acres acquired through the program.

Professor Dennison was also coach of the golf team. By my senior year, because of the war, there were hardly enough good players left to make up a team. All of the players were fraternity brothers or good friends of mine. I was a terrible golfer, but I saw an opportunity to spend spring afternoons on the golf course rather than in a lab. I convinced Professor Dennison that he needed a reserve golfer who could drive the van to matches and play if anyone were sick. My friends helped convince him that I could play in a pinch. The only problem was that there was a mandatory foundry and machine shop lab course that I was supposed to take. I told Professor Dennison that I had spent two summers working at Columbus Iron Works, which was true, and that there was little new that I could learn from the course. I asked him if I could substitute a course in time and motion study, and he agreed. I had a glorious time the spring of my senior year playing golf with my buddies, and although I never came close to playing a match, I did take several nice trips with good friends.

A month before graduation I was convinced that I would graduate, so I mailed out invitations to relatives and friends, and then the ax fell. Dean Skiles called me into his office and told me I couldn't graduate because I hadn't completed the required course in foundry and machine shop. Dean Skiles wore a hearing aid with a receiver pinned to his vest, and when he wished to end a conversation, he would turn the receiver off and turn around to his desk. I pled my case before him, but when I saw him reach for the "off" switch, I knew my goose was cooked. I went to see Professor Dennison, and he agreed to go to bat for me. When he returned, he told me that he had assumed full responsibility for the mistake and if I could build the required electric motor in the three weeks remaining, Dean Skiles would give me a "D" in the course and allow me to graduate.

I had to complete a semester course in three weeks. Basically, I had to make engineering drawings, interpret the drawings, make patterns and molds, cast and machine the molds, machine the shaft and end bell caps, wind and assemble the motor, and maintain my other courses all in three weeks. And the motor had to run!

I started to work, and everyone in the shop sympathized with me and wanted me to succeed. Two days before the deadline I plugged my finished motor in, and it ran! There was just one little snag: it ran backward. I had wound it wrong. Thinking quickly, I said to the head of the shop, "Look, if I cross the pulley belt, it will run in the right direction." He laughed and said, "Get out of here. You've got your 'D'." I gave the motor to my brother-in-law, Clarence Butler, and he used it in his shop for a number of years.

While at Tech I made the swim team and swam competitively. I'd been playing freshman basketball, and a friend and I decided to go in the pool one day. The coach saw me swimming and asked me to swim against one of his dashers, and I beat him. So he asked me to go out for the team, and I did. I knew just looking at the times of the other team's swimmers that there were people out there better than I was. In the first three or four meets, coaches from the other schools would put their second man against me and their best swimmer against our guy swimming the 200. I was swimming the dash—50-yard and the 100-yard—thinking the second man would beat me. Well, he wouldn't beat me. I went through that every week, though knowing in my heart that I was going to lose. I couldn't take it. It was drudgery for me to get out there to practice and compete.

I told the coach, "This is tearing me up. My stomach is cramping, and I can't sleep." He said, "Listen, if you didn't have that adrenaline flowing like that, you couldn't beat anybody. You ought to be thankful that you can get that pumped up." I started getting some sinus trouble and decided I'd quit, but the main reason I quit was fear of failure. I couldn't handle it. I don't know that I ever really thought about what would happen to me if I lost. I had just been conditioned that you didn't fail. I've fallen on my face a hundred times since, but back then it was something I just couldn't handle. Plus, I was having a good time at Tech. Laying around the pool was more fun than competitive swimming.

A great surprise to me was being elected president of my college fraternity while still a junior. This was the first time that someone realized I might have leadership ability, unless you count the time my peers elected me bathroom captain in the third grade at Wynnton School.

Still, I yearned for approval. Growing up, I had tried to do many things to make my parents proud of me. Later as a teenager, I did the same thing with my peers to win their approval. Unfortunately, the things that my peers approved were 180 degrees from what was approved by my parents. In the Navy I made a commitment to myself to be the best, and I finished near the top of my class, after finishing near the bottom of my class in college. In both cases the focus was on approval of different groups, not on learning. Later in business I was a poor manager because I put too much emphasis on wanting the respect of others.

During those years I was playing a role, and I knew it. We have been taught since childhood to wear masks. If you hurt, don't cry. If you are afraid, try to hide it. If you are empty and lonely, smile. If you are helpless, pretend to be strong. But when a person discovers self-worth, he begins to ask himself the question, "How can I really know if anyone loves me as long as I wear a mask and am a phony? How can I know whether they love me or whether they love what I pretend to be?"

I didn't feel real because I was too busy living up to everyone else's perception of who I should be. With my parents and church members I was "Mr. Clean." But with my friends at Georgia Tech I was a "legend in my own mind." Neither of those images was what I felt I was—a scared, inadequate little boy who had never grown up. Today I no longer do things to win approval of others, but I probably do them to win approval from myself. Yet I know God loves me "in spite of," not "because of."

I am not proud of the way I acted during my college years, and I realize that I was very fortunate that nothing bad happened to me and that there were no bad lasting effects of my irresponsible behavior.

Maxims Handed Down by W. C. Bradley

In 1935, the W. C. Bradley Company celebrated its 50th year in business in Columbus. In honor of the occasion, someone put together a collection of memories. Included in the collection were a number of sayings that my grandfather used frequently. I include those here:

- The secret to my success is the Golden Rule: Do unto others as you would have others do unto you.
- Keep on keeping on.
- Be sure you're right; then go ahead.
- Keep your average good.
- I don't worry about God Almighty's business.
- The man doesn't live who doesn't make mistakes.
- I won't do that! I've got to sleep with myself.
- Most people worry about things that never happen.
- Write people's virtues on a table of stone and their faults on the sands of the seashore.
- Deader than a mackerel.
- Quicker than a minnow can swim a branch.
- Don't let them get you in the nine hole.
- To make a man trustworthy, you must first trust him.
- That would cost enough money to burn up a wet dog.
- Let'em skin their own skunk.
- It's as sound as a hound's tooth.
- You've got to make your bread and molasses match.
- Honesty is the best policy, leaving the moral question out of it.
- Don't give a competitor a soot bag with which to beat you over the head.

Elizabeth Bradley Turner was a woman of exceptional grace and beauty who taught her children a love of nature and always to "do the right thing."

CHAPTER 3

THE NAVY—
A CALL TO SERVE

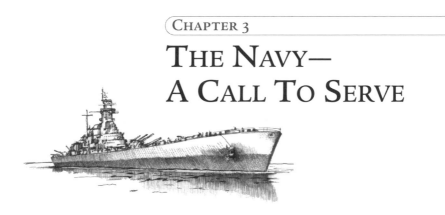

It costs so much to be a full human being that there are very few who have the enlightenment, or the courage, to pay the price . . . One has to abandon altogether the search for security, and reach out to the risk of living with both arms. One has to embrace the world like a lover, and yet demand no easy return of love. One has to accept pain as a condition of existence. One has to court doubt and darkness as the cost of knowing. One needs a will stubborn in conflict, but apt always to the total acceptance of every consequence of living and dying.[4]

—Morris West

Everyone has pivotal events in their lives. One of the first significant ones for me was when I joined the Navy in 1943. I have always loved the water and felt at home in it. I learned to swim at age two by crawling on the bottom of my grandfather's pool. I think my love for the water had something to do with my choice of the Navy for service in World War II.

At Georgia Tech I took Navy ROTC and thought of going into the service as a glamorous thing to do. Movies had brainwashed us and, being young, we were highly susceptible to their influence. So much of the volunteering was grounded in the movies. I thought Cary Grant looked better in a Navy uniform than Spencer Tracy looked in an Army uniform.

I first went to Midshipman's School at Columbia University. While there I stayed on the fourth floor in John Jay Hall and had to run up four flights of steps at least five times a day. I got in great physical condition. I graduated in the top 10 percent of the class and was assigned to a destroyer escort, a ship smaller than a destroyer and the one I had requested. Then I went to Key West station for antisubmarine warfare training, and I believe an incident that occurred there resulted in a minesweep assignment.

One of my best friends was a good baseball player, and Key West, Florida, prided itself in its Navy baseball team. My friend had played at the University of Pennsylvania and had a contract to play with the New York Yankees. He and I went to the officers' club one day, met two girls there, and hired a taxi to take us to where one of the girls lived. We didn't know until we got there that she was the commandant's daughter. It wasn't until they told us good night and went inside that we realized we didn't know how we were going to get back to the base. We spotted two bicycles leaning against a shed, and we must have been talking pretty loud because the commandant called the shore patrol. Well, we were running from the shore patrol on the bicycles, and my friend ran into a clotheslines and got caught. I ran my bicycle up against a cyclone fence, jumped it, and made it back to the base. After that, my orders were changed. My friend played baseball the rest of the war, and I got sent to fight.

I was ordered to Tampa, Florida, and assigned to a minesweeper, the AM 220. From there I was sent to Little Creek, Virginia, for minesweeper training "shakedown." While there I took some frogman training because I had been on Tech's swimming team and thought that being a frogman might be as glamorous as it was in the movies.

I enjoyed the Navy, but several incidents probably kept me from pursuing it as a career. One day our young officers were practicing ship handling out in the harbor by docking the ship alongside the buoys. When we started to the real dock, the skipper said, "Let me show you how to make a destroyer landing." So he went barreling into the dock at full speed. When he called for "all engines reverse," the engine room called the bridge and said, "We can't reverse. These young guys have used up all the air we use to brake the engines." So we went barreling into the dock, taking out a good piece of it. Fortunately, our ship was sturdy enough to escape serious damage.

Another incident occurred while we were practicing simulated submarine runs. A tugboat was playing the part of the submarine, and as anti-submarine warfare officer, I was in control of the attacks. We attacked subs by sending out a sound wave—a "ping"—and if the echo came back, we could locate the sub and the frequency pitch of the returning echo to determine the direction the sub was heading (known as the Doppler Effect). Because I had good pitch differentiation, I was good at attacking subs. The skipper wanted the attack to be realistic, so he ordered the sailors to arm the K-guns used to fire depth charges. I had checked to be sure that the switch that fired the K-guns was off. Just before I completed the run, though, the captain came into the ASDIC hut and flipped the switch, thinking he was turning it off. When I pushed the button, there was a horrible explosion, and I came out of the ASDIC hut just in time to see a perfect pattern of depth charges bracket the tugboat. When the people on the tugboat realized what was happening, they went to "general quarters," meaning that they battened down the hatches and took to battle stations with their life jackets on because they knew the end was near. Fortunately, the depth charges were set at a point greater than the depth of the water, so they didn't explode. Someone had to retrieve the charges. The captain is probably still writing reports trying to explain how this happened.

Our skipper's fate was probably sealed, though, the day I made a run on a whale shortly after going through the Panama Canal on the way to Pearl Harbor. Unfortunately, he had radioed that we were attacking a sub and had to explain why we blew up a whale instead of a submarine.

Then there was the great pumpkin pie caper. The junior officer, the lowest officer on the totem pole, was the commissary officer in charge of the cooks. He was the one that everybody griped to about the food. I was the commissary officer, in addition to my other duties as submarine warfare officer and gunnery officer. Before we left for Pearl Harbor, we went to pick up supplies, and a guy said, "You're going out there to the war zone, and Thanksgiving and Christmas are coming.

Load up on pumpkin pies and cans of mincemeat, and you'll be the biggest hero in the war. You can pull alongside every ship, and you can trade those for steaks, chicken, and fresh vegetables." So I loaded up on pumpkin pies and mincemeat. I mean I loaded up. When we got out there, we'd pull alongside another ship and before we could say a word they'd say, "You want some pumpkin pies?" This guy had loaded every ship with pumpkin pies. We had mincemeat and pumpkin pie three times a day until we ate it up. After that, I was relieved of my duty as commissary officer (probably because of a threatened mutiny by the crew) and was made a gunnery officer in charge of anti-aircraft defense. There my hunting experience increased my proficiency.

Another time, "general quarters" sounded in the middle of the night. I was slow getting out of the bed, I guess, and trying to get my helmet on. I started up the ladder, but just as I reached the top, they slammed the hatch down to make the ship waterproof. It knocked me down the ladder. I got up groggy and went to my station. Of course, I was directing fire control that day. Man, I was doing a terrific job. We were shooting things down, and I was telling them which way to go and what to do. When we got through, I discovered my headset wasn't even plugged in.

I was in the Navy for three years and stayed at sea for a year once, if you don't count going to port for repairs and supplies. While at sea, we stood four hours on watch and eight hours off, unless we were at "general quarters" where everyone was on station. That routine allowed much time for reflection. Standing watch at night, I was awed by the vastness and the rhythm of the universe. When I wanted to know where I was, I took a fix on the stars, and they were always where they were supposed to be. The sun came up when it was supposed to come up, and the tide moved when it was supposed to move. It gave me a sense that somebody was in charge and in control of it.

I learned to love and respect the ocean. I loved being at sea. I'd see little birds flying thousands of miles from shore, and they'd light on my ship, catch their breath, and then fly on. I loved being told where to go, not having to make decisions. I loved having a common goal that everybody worked toward. I'd have stayed in the Navy, I think, if I hadn't had something to draw me back home. Even today I love everything about the sea. I can go to the beach and get into a rhythm that slows down my clock to nothing. I love the surf. The sea is my friend. People worry about undertows. If you get into an undertow and you don't fight it and swim to the side of it, the sea will bring you back to shore.

One of the best things that happened to me is that I started to read when I was at sea. Out of sheer boredom I read every book in the ship's library, ending with Will Durant's *Story of Philosophy*,[5] which opened a new world to me. That book stirred me to begin a quest to find out what life was all about, who we are, why we're here, and what makes us unique.

I saw a good bit of action in Guam, Saipan, Iwo Jima, Okinawa, and the Philippines. But I wanted to spare my parents the fear of knowing that I was in the fighting. I had told them that my ship was stationed in the Aleutian Islands (Alaska), when I was really in the South Pacific. One day at mail call a box from my mother arrived, and everyone gathered around to share the cookies they thought were inside. What I pulled out of the box was a heavy wool ski mask and mittens that my mother had knitted for me to protect me from the Arctic winds. Shortly after that, my parents saw a picture of my ship in the Okinawa invasion, and the jig was up.

My time in the Navy was one of tremendous personal growth. I knew I was out from under the spotlight. But the main thing I realized was that whatever happened wasn't because of my family. I was on my own. I began to experience, for the first time, an appreciation and respect for myself out of the framework of the family. And being in the presence of death quite often caused me to think about the meaning of life. I didn't know at the time that I had already been "stamped for redemption" (Eph 1:13-14) and that there is an emptiness in each of us that demands we find some meaning to our existence. But I knew that a good part of me was phony, pretending to be good when I wasn't.

The way I handled the stress of war was to imagine that I was the star in some movie. Back then the star, the hero, in war movies never got killed. Even today when I think about the war, I really can't distinguish between fantasy and fact, nor do I want to. I have learned since then that many people who undergo posttraumatic stress resort to this pattern. I do know that I was in some pretty hairy situations for three years and that we got a presidential unit citation for our ship's part in one of the invasions. By the grace of God I came through those situations intact. Many of my friends and classmates didn't. I pray that my children and grandchildren don't ever have to go through the horrors of war. It was a time of great growth for me, but there are far better ways to grow.

Bill Turner, in khaki, and the crew of the *USS Device AM 220* receive the Presidential Unit Citation for their role in World War II.

This is one of the things I think I did. We were sweeping mines in the Philippines, and I was talking semaphor to this friend on one of the other ships. While we were talking, his ship hit a mine, and I don't know whether I dreamed this or not, but I think I saw a man on the flying bridge go all the way up into the air, almost to the mast. The ship sank. Ships sweep in formation, so the ship behind us went to their rescue and also hit a mine. Our captain wanted to do something to get those people out of the water, so we put out whaleboats. I volunteered to take one of the whaleboats in and went through the minefield and picked up survivors and brought them back to the ship. I remember putting them on the deck in the mess hall. They were all in shock, and we just routinely gave them a shot of morphine. We didn't have any doctors on the ship, just a pharmacist's mate. Then we called the destroyer to come get the wounded. I think that's real, but I'm not sure. It's like it happened to somebody else. That's the way I got through it. You just do what you've got to do and get through it the best way you can.

I really feel for those guys who fought in the Vietnam War, who came home to derision and criticism. What they experienced was so much worse than what I went through because those who fought in World War II were heroes and everybody liked what we were doing.

We were in Okinawa Harbor, just south of Japan, sweeping the East China Sea for the invasion of Japan at the time we learned the war was over. Everybody started shooting flares and rockets to celebrate. I didn't know it at the time, but I got a piece of shrapnel through my jaw, a small piece that the dentist found 15-20 years after I got out of the Navy.

One thing I learned in the Navy was to think ahead for all possible situations that might develop and plan the solutions to any problems well in advance of their happening. The officers who had the best reputations for "coolness under fire" were good planners for how to cope with what might develop. Officers who did not have this "coolness" were said to operate under the adage "when in trouble or in doubt, run in circles, scream, and shout."

Experience also plays a role in good decision making. I can remember being in a typhoon in Okinawa and taking shelter in a harbor called Kerrama Rhetto. When the storm hit, we were going backwards, in spite of the fact that we had two anchors out and our engines were going ahead flank speed. It was awesome, and it did considerable damage to our ship. We learned the lesson the hard way. The next time a typhoon hit, we elected to go to sea, put the storm on our quarter, and move around the storm. Even storms have a pattern. We had a lot of seasickness, but no damage.

You also learn in advance that there is less chance of being hit if you turn toward a torpedo or a mine once it clears the ship's turning axis. You learn that in a kamikaze attack there is less chance of being hit if you fire sporadically rather than a steady fire that allows the plane to come down the tracer path.

These same principles apply to business and community relationships. You learn that there is less danger if you turn toward problems with solutions rather than try to avoid them. Wayne Gretzky, the great hockey player, said that the secret of his success is that he skates to where the puck is going to be.

As the war ended, our ship was ordered to Sasebo, Japan to be a part of the occupational force. One of the things that impressed me was that there were no dogs or cats on the streets. We were told that the people had eaten them all. Along the dock where our ship was moored were many "entrepreneurs" wanting to exchange jewelry, pearls, and Japanese war memorabilia for cigarettes. Soon after the occupation, the U.S. established a "point system" that enabled service-men with the most points to return to civilian life. This was a chaotic time on board our ship because neither the existing skipper nor his successor would authorize my release because I was one of the few experienced officers left.

Our ship soon received orders to return to the states, along with other ships. At the convoy-forming meetings we were asked if anyone there had experience as a navigator. Sitting on the front row, I held up my hand, not knowing that I was the only candidate to pilot 20 ships back to the states. That didn't bother me too much until I returned to my ship to learn that my chief quartermaster assistant had been trans-ferred. I could "shoot" the stars with my sextant, and I could do the necessary calculations to plot our position, but the assistant was the only one who could identify the stars, and I had to know that in order to do the calculations.

I could identify the sun and shoot the sun to get a sun line and I could identify the North Star (Polaris), which could give us our lati-tude. With that meager knowledge, plus dead reckoning, our 20 ships set off for San Diego. I will admit that "dead reckoning" took on new meaning for me!

When I went into the service, I had told my dad that I did not want him in any way to try to influence the duty I might be assigned because I couldn't handle it if someone died in my place. He honored my request, but when I saw that my release might be held up because the new skipper coming on board would not approve my request, I wrote him that he was free to pull any strings he could to get me out. When we reached San Diego, my orders were waiting to proceed to Charleston to take command of an experimental landing craft to be delivered to Green Cove Springs, Florida, for decommissioning. I don't know which caused me the most relief—finding San Diego or knowing I would soon be out of the Navy!

There was only one problem. There were no navigational charts of the Inland Waterway in Charleston. So in frustration I found a Texaco road map, and with it and a skeleton crew aboard we took off for the promised land! The trip down the Inland Waterway to Green Cove Springs was relaxing and fun, and we arrived without any major mishaps, except that I began to experience all the symptoms of appendicitis. I had experienced one previous attack while at sea and had kept the pharmacist mate at bay with my .45 automatic lest he do anything more than bring me an ice pack. He had visions of being famous for operating at sea, and he had all the "how-to" drawings in hand.

I was relieved of command and transferred to the Navy hospital in Jacksonville where I had emergency surgery under an epidural anesthesia because of my desire to be in control. The appendectomy actually expedited my release, and I was soon out of the Navy and back on my way to civilian life.

Thoughts While Passing Through

- Excuses are a form of self-justification, and self-justification is a form of self-worship.
- Even when you can't enjoy yourself, you can enjoy someone else.
- The big choices have always been easy for me. There were times when I have had to lay my life on the line for what I believe. If you are afraid to die for what you believe, then you're already dead. I wonder what would happen if I made the little choices with the same conviction.
- If my main concern was to keep my car from being scratched, I would leave it in the garage.
- It is much better to be afraid with others than to be afraid of others.

CHAPTER 4

LEARNING
THROUGH LOVE

When I was 19, my dad and I went to Golden Park to a baseball game. In a box across from us was a pretty little blond-haired, brown-eyed, twelve-year-old girl sitting with her father. I distinctly remember thinking, "That's the girl I'm going to marry someday." What I didn't know then was that she was thinking a similar thought about me. The girl was Sue Marie Thompson, the daughter of John Barkwell Thompson Jr.—a very successful ear, eye, nose, and throat specialist in Columbus—and Mildred Marie Dykes—a homemaker.

Her parents were handsome people and were considered a model couple. Both were from Cochran, Georgia, and moved to Columbus after Dr. Thompson's graduation from Emory Medical School and some early experience with Dr. Wise's Clinic in Plains, Georgia. Sue Marie's brother, John Daniel Thompson, is her only sibling. He served as head of the obstetrics/gynecology department at Emory Medical School for a number of years and is a renowned gynecologist who has given talks and lectures all over the world.

After my graduation from midshipman's school, I visited my sister, Betty, at Wesleyan College. Hearing giggling from an upstairs window as I stood outside, I looked up to see Sue Marie pointing me out to her friends. When I returned to Columbus after the war, I kept my eye on her, but was too shy to make a move.

In 1948 I finally got up the nerve to break in on her at a dance. She loves to tell people that I was shaking like a leaf—probably war nerves. By October of that year we were married—from Golden Park to Golden Pond with six children and 21 grands along the way. The grands had the good sense to name her "Precious," which she is.

Bill and Sue Marie Turner on their wedding day, October 8, 1948. More than 50 years later, Bill calls Sue Marie his "best friend."

Keeping me on track was only one part of the difficult task that Sue Marie took on when she said "yes" to our life together when she was barely 19. In short order she became pregnant with our first child. Donna Sue Turner (Brown) was delivered ten months after our wedding. Both sets of grandparents breathed a sign of relief that the baby didn't come sooner.

We built a big house and five other children followed about two years apart: William Bradley "Brad" Turner Jr., Marie Dykes Turner (Moshell), John Thompson Turner, Sarah Hall "Sallie" Turner (Martin), and Don Abbott Turner II. Someone once asked Sue Marie, after remarking on our large family, if she were Catholic, and she replied, "No, I'm just a sexy Methodist."

While I have felt like I am on a journey of self-discovery, Sue Marie has always known who she is—a dutiful and loving wife, a fierce mother, and a homemaker. Our early years together were turbulent because I was preoccupied with becoming what others expected me to be, and then, when I accepted Christ at age 32, it became even more difficult for her. I became involved in Faith at Work and the Lay Witness movement. Like a dutiful wife, she tried to come along, but the whole experience was disturbing and threatening to her. It was made worse when I told her that as I understood the Bible, God had to come first in my life, and she and the family were second. What a dumb thing to tell a young wife with a big house full of small children!

In the early years of marriage you wonder why somebody is not like you. Later, I think you appreciate the fact that they aren't, that together you make up a whole. I once prayed that God would change Sue Marie so that she would be like me, and I received an answer to that prayer. What I think God said to me loud and clear was that what happens between Sue Marie and me is our business, but I must concentrate on my relationship with Him and what He wants me to be.

Despite my shortcomings, Sue Marie stuck by me, giving me from her heart what I needed most—unconditional love. Before Sue Marie, I thought people loved me only when I performed well. I couldn't even imagine someone loving me just because I am. My dad loved me. There's no question in my mind that he loved me, but the way he showed it was by saying, "I'm proud of you." When I scored 20 points in a basketball game, that's when I got praise. That was performance. I grew up thinking I had to perform to be worthwhile, to be loved. My dad's generation, particularly men, just didn't show feelings. Men did not talk to their sons about things like love. My mother always praised me by saying, "You always do the right thing." When I didn't do the "right thing," she acted hurt and like a martyr because I didn't respond properly to all the good things she did for me. She could send me on a guilt trip when I let her down. When I became angry when I was little, she made me read all the scriptures in the Bible about anger. I learned many good things from her, but I also learned to hide my feelings.

When you are a seeker of love and you think behavior is the determining factor, you're lost. You are in a box. It's not real, and somehow you know it's not real. You just don't have the freedom to get out and be who you really are.

I remember being in the hospital in Naples, Florida, after a boating accident that nearly severed my foot. My friends took me to the hospital and stayed with me through surgery, but left while I was in recovery after the doctors told them I was okay. I remember thinking, "If I fall off this stretcher, no one cares enough to pick me up," and I gripped the rails of the stretcher, fighting for control. I had that same fight for control in the Navy when I had my appendectomy with a spinal block instead of general anesthesia.

I know now that the real fear was not about losing control. It was fear of not being loved. Tied into that was also a lack of trust. First John 4 says perfect love casts out fear, and although I'm not there yet, I know that it does. If you fix your eye on the goal, being tackled, even stomped, is not going to keep you from getting up and running the ball one more time—and you'll try to run it a little smarter, better, and harder next time! But it's also important to listen to what the coach has to say.

Sue Marie was my liberation from the box I put myself in. What started the change in me was her unconditional love. She let me know that I was a mess, but I was her mess, and she loved me anyhow. Later I discovered that God loves me in the same way. When people find love and acceptance, they are willing to take an honest look at themselves and begin to grow and change. When people develop a sense of self-worth based on who they are (God's children) rather than what they do, they can go to God in prayer and look through God's eyes at themselves.

I've grown to know that in my own family it is not when I pretend to be the omnipotent, successful, attractive father and husband that I really know love. It's when my family sees me in all of my meanness, littleness, and pettiness and still reaches out to me in love that I really know what love is all about. Experiencing this love made me want to risk being vulnerable and transparent to others in order to discover an even greater love. I began to discover a reciprocal openness on the part of others that shows how love works. I also began to minister to the little child that exists in me and to fulfill my great need, not only to be caring, but to be cared for.

Sue Marie was the first one who could make me look at myself and see what I was. She made me realize that I do things to get approval. There was a time in my life, for instance, when I felt like I had to do anything people asked me to do. If I turned people down, I had to make some elaborate excuse as to why I couldn't do what they asked. It's only been in the last five or six years that I could say, "No, I don't want to do that. I don't feel right about it, or I don't have anything to say on that subject." I'm often asked to speak at civic functions. Today, if I've got something to say, I'll speak, but I don't just get up and talk because someone wants me to talk. It has taken me a long time to get to this point. I wanted people to approve of me and think well of me. I don't have to do that any more. It's real liberating to get to a point of not having to explain your actions to anybody. That is a major priority with me now.

Sue Marie was also the first one to encourage me to express myself. She was raised very differently from me. Her family was full of love, but they exploded. If something happened that they didn't like, they would just go at it. They let it out, and it was all over. When we first got married and she started doing that, I said, "Whoa, wait a minute. What in the world have I gotten myself into?" My parents didn't do that. In my family you didn't make waves. I never saw my parents fight. They probably closed the door and had discussions, but I never saw them scream and holler. It was a learning experience for me. It felt uncomfortable. I wasn't used to it, and Sue Marie and I went through some tough times because of it. But it's the way to go. I don't have any doubt about that.

One of the great lessons Sue Marie has taught me, our family, and others is never to stop loving. She reminds me of the story of the little boy with such emotional and behavioral problems that psychologists had given up on him. One day someone gave him a puppy. The boy sat on the back step, and every time the puppy tried to get close to him, the boy kicked him down the steps. Finally, after the tenth kick, the boy went to his mother with a look of wonder on his face, a smile on his lips, and the puppy held closely in his arms. "Mommy, no matter how many times I try to hurt him, he still loves me." Sue Marie is like that puppy. No matter how much she is hurt or rejected, she still reaches out in love and eventually wins the other person over.

Sue Marie has outgrown me. She was probably always a better person than I am, but there is no doubt now that she is. She is the most thoughtful, caring person I have ever known. She always does the right, loving thing, and most of the time sees that I do the same. She once told me that as part of her church visitation, she was going to the hospital to see a 98-year-old man she didn't know. My first reaction was, "He'll never know you are there." She responded "He's lonely, and he'll know someone cares," and she went and held his hand. This is what Jesus had in mind when he said, "The greatest shall be a servant."

Sue Marie has been my touchstone when I veered off from what was real. I wish I had a dime for every time in my life that she has told me, "You are not facing reality." I read somewhere that when Mahatma Gandhi returned from a triumphant tour, he always went to his spinning wheel. That was the way he kept his perspective of who he was. It is easy for someone in a leadership position, as I have been, to begin to think they are omnipotent. That happened to me as those who worked with me told me how smart I was. In addition, there were many well-meaning organizations that wanted me to receive an award at their fundraising dinners. That was pretty heady stuff for someone like me who had a large ego and a need for the approval of others. Sue Marie is my "spinning wheel" who keeps me in touch with who I am.

Marriage, I think, is about learning—learning to communicate from your deepest heart, learning to forgive by knowing you are the kind of person who has received forgiveness, and learning to give and accept unconditional love. Marriage is not about learning to get your own needs met.

One habit Sue Marie and I formed early in our marriage was having a "date" at least once a week. This was a time when we really listened to each other, since most of our conversations at home were contests over family issues.

Our children filled our lives in ways I can't explain. I don't think I was all that bad a father. I spent a good bit of time with my kids, coaching Little League for nine years, teaching them to hunt, attending their recitals and things like that, but I wanted to be their pal, and not their parent, and I left all of the tough parenting to Sue Marie. She let me know that this was just another manifestation of my need for approval.

At Sue Marie's insistence I learned to do my share of the disciplining. My kids' recollection is that every night when I came home, I would go into the room where they watched television and say to one or all of them, "Do you want your spanking before or after Superman?"

Dr. Benjamin Spock was the expert when we began our family, and it seems to me that experts change theories on child-raising almost as often as nutritionists change theories on what foods are good for us. We made every mistake parents could make. There were many stormy times in our family. Our kids were far from perfect, and we have had our share of tragedy and catastrophic experiences.

Our children, whom we call the "fourth generation," are all in the same family, and yet they are all as different as night and day. Donna at a very early age assumed the responsibility of being the "little mother" to her siblings. She is still doing this in her own family and in her Atlanta community. She and her husband, David, are very supportive of their children and spend much time with them. The courageous way that David and Donna faced the loss of their baby son and the love and commitment they have shown to their children—Cameron, McKnight, and Jay—have been an inspiration to all our family.

Brad, who is now president and chief operating officer of the W. C. Bradley Company, has always, very quietly, done his own thing in his own way. He is a champion of the underdog and cares very deeply about people. He often solicits my help in causes where he is committed. Brad views the world through glasses that allow him to see the humor in most situations. He has a wonderful ability to laugh at himself. His sensitivity to other people develops the trust that is essential to leadership. He and his wife, Sally, have four children: Bill, Jack, Bobsie, and Millie.

Our daughter, Marie, has a strong, tough, stubborn will that has enabled her to recover from her husband's death and do a remarkable job raising her three children, Turner, Lane, and Sue Marie. A tower of strength for her children, she only calls us when she really needs us. She serves on the board of the Pastoral Institute.

John is very competitive and likes a challenge. In his early years he loved to engage me in debate. It didn't matter the subject or which side he took, he just liked to argue. After college graduation he was considering law school, but I asked him to join the company and develop a mail order business, now Bradley Direct. He later moved on to other responsibilities. He is engaged in helping form our family office, which will have the mission of managing our family plans and instilling our family traditions, heritage, and values in the next generation. Whatever John takes on, whether it be family, business, community, or sports, he always does it with a great passion to win and be the best. John's wife, Amandah, is working on a Ph.D. in family counseling. They have three children: Gardiner, Thompson, and Rion.

Sallie is our lightning rod. She's the one whom other members of the family use to vent their anger, frustration, and other feelings. We know it's safe with Sallie. We know she can take it, most of the time with good humor. We also know that she will continue to love us. She, like John, is competitive and frequently overloads herself with community activities. Sallie and her husband, John Martin, make a good team, and their different personalities complement each other and help them in raising their children: Katie, Elizabeth, Lulie, and John.

Abbott left school early to get married, but has trained himself to be a great communicator and a good manager, skills that are extremely valuable in his position as vice president of human resources for Char-Broil. He has done well at every task given to him and has unlimited potential. He and his wife, Cathey, have four children: Clark, Abbott, Ashley, and Brooke.

As adults, our children and their spouses are wonderful parents and contribute in a substantial and fruitful way to their world. We are proud and grateful for each of them. I think what saved them was a mother who wouldn't give up, who taught them and me the meaning of love.

Our family has had its moments, many of them chaotic. I'll never forget the trip we took out west in our station wagon with our six children, the oldest about 16 at the time. It was, without doubt, the trip from hell. It took two weeks, but it seemed like a lot longer than that. We went to Phoenix, the Grand Canyon, New Mexico, Los Angeles, San Francisco, Modesto Valley, and Yosemite National Park. The only thing I remember about that trip is that I would drive 200 miles, and when I stopped, all four doors of the car exploded, and everybody came out swinging at everybody else. Brad was picking on John, and John was picking on Abbott. One of them would say, "Marie is touching me." We'd ride through the Redwood Forest and say, "Isn't this magnificent?" and they'd say, "What's on at the picture show?" Ask my children what they remember about that trip, and they'll say that every day I'd say, "We're going home tomorrow." I meant it too.

There are things I would do differently if I could do it over again. I would let my children see me as I really am, warts and all. I would love their mother more in front of them. And I would listen better to what they had to say.

In 1998, the year Sue Marie and I celebrated our 50th anniversary, I asked her what she would like as an anniversary gift. She immediately said, "I want to take our entire family on a cruise." We all had taken an Alaskan cruise together two years before, and our children had taken us all to Jackson Hole, Wyoming, the next year, and both of those were marvelous experiences. But I must admit I had some reservations about pushing our luck a third time. To me, the idea of 34 people ages 7 months to 75 years being cooped up together on a ship could get dicey, but with some anxiety I told her to go ahead and plan the trip. We spent 10 days together cruising around Scotland, playing golf, and sightseeing at each port. Scotland is a beautiful country.

But to me the highlight of the trip was our evening meals. We had five tables together in one corner of the dining room, and sitting back and seeing these beautiful people interact, relate, and love each other brought tears of joy to my eyes every evening. In addition to being family, my children and grandchildren are best friends, and as I looked around the room I could not help but think, "This is what life is all about." Anything I have accomplished pales when placed next to this.

I don't claim to be an expert on family bliss. My family knows me best, and it is here that I fail the most to be what I should be. But it is also here where I find the most unconditional love and where the lessons of 1 John can best be learned. Through the experience that years bring, I've learned some things about the dynamics of family relationships, and I've tried to use what I've learned in helping my Sunday School kids relate to their parents. When I talk to them about it, I call it a "mini-course in family relations." What I tell them is:

- Model what you wish to see happen. The basic desire of all relationships is the desire for love, acceptance, openness, trust, and honesty. Ask yourself if you are bringing this to your relationships.

- Be sure that all your actions, verbal and nonverbal, build self-worth for each person, including yourself. This means no blame, no advice, and no judgment.

- Be sure that you are separating the behavior—which may be bad—from the person—who is always good. When you do this, you can begin to discover the "why" in the behavior.

- Don't accumulate resentment until you explode. Handle and resolve each issue as it comes up.

- You cannot force a change in someone's behavior. But when a person finds unconditional love and understanding, the person will change.

- Learn to listen effectively. Mirror the other person's feelings with statements such as "Did I understand you to say . . ." and "I hear . . .". Learn to listen between the lines for what is not said. Remember that the need behind all communication is, "I want to know that you care." If communication begins to break down, have each person repeat what the other said to the other's satisfaction before responding. Many times we are so busy thinking of what we will say next, we fail to listen.

- Avoid "you" statements and "why" questions; they make the other person defensive. Make "I" statements: "I feel . . ." or "I need . . .".

- When you become angry, realize that anger usually comes from other feelings such as fear, embarrassment, frustration, inadequacy, and jealousy. Take time to discover the cause of your anger. Another person may trigger your anger, but he/she does not cause it.

- A good strategy for conflict resolution is: (1) Define the problem to the satisfaction of both, deciding who "owns" the problem. Identify the values involved, if possible; for if value conflict is involved, resolution is most difficult, if not impossible. Be sure your values are consistent with your behavior. (2) Begin conflict resolution with prayer, holding hands, But be careful not to preach at each other. Psalm 139 is a good beginning point for prayer. (3) Negotiate a contract where neither loses, both win, and all commit to live up to the contract. This will build the self-esteem needed to cause change in behavior.

• Conclude communication with a hug. A hug is worth 1,000 words. It says: "I love you," "Forgive me," "I forgive you." Continue to hug until all tension goes out of both parties.

I know I often fall short of these rules for constructive communication. Sometimes it's good to have a referee/coach to keep dialogue on track.

In raising my own children and working with the teenagers in my Sunday School class, I've defined some goals that I think are important for parents to instill in children. As I thought about it, I realized these are goals all of us can use, goals for children of all ages:

• Have a right relationship with God because this is the source of all love.

• Develop self-esteem that comes through realizing you are a unique, one-of-a-kind child of God and that you are loved unconditionally. It is important to really listen to what a child has to say before responding. Proverbs 18:13 says, "If anyone answers before he hears, it is his folly and shame." I never offer advice because advice sends the message, "You're not capable of deciding for yourself." A better approach is to look at options and consequences together and then let the other person choose their course of action.

• Be the same person in all circumstances. That's the only way to know real love.

• Show feelings constructively because we either feel everything, or eventually we become depressed or feel nothing at all. We can't feel selectively for very long. Feelings come in layers. For example, beneath anger there is usually fear.

- View yourself as a student of life rather than as a victim. We all experience pain. There are three things we can do with pain: We can nurse it, we can rehearse it, or we can immerse it in service to others.

I've had another model of the perfect relationship. Sue Marie calls her the "other woman" in my life. She has soft brown eyes that can communicate without speaking. She has long brown hair tinted with red that other women would kill for. She is a great partner, ready to do whatever I wish with great enthusiasm. She is a wonderful hunting and fishing companion who loves to see me succeed, keeps her mouth shut when I fail, and communicates that we will do better next time. The only problem is that when we fish, she becomes so excited when I catch something that she scares the other fish away and we have to move to another part of the lake. I can always count on her being delighted to see me, and, if given half a chance, she will be in my lap, cuddling close. She trusts me completely.

Her real name is Turner's Classic Coke, but everyone calls her Cokie. She is a Boykin Spaniel, who Sue Marie and I both believe is God's gift of love to us. Both of us believe she loves us the best—and so does Frank who works for us. If ever Cokie doesn't do exactly what we say, it's because she doesn't understand.

Cokie is getting old. She is blind, but I don't mind being a seeing-eye man. She is also deaf and has a terrible allergic skin condition that becomes infected easily. She eats very little and lies around all day, and she doesn't understand all of the things I have to do like stuffing pills down her throat and cleaning her ears. Cokie was a gift to us from Ben Hardaway, but is probably one of the most expensive dogs ever because of her medication and treatment. We are glad to pay for her treatment, but we are beginning to understand that somewhere in the future we may be faced with a hard decision of what is really best for her. I'm not sure I can make the decision to end her suffering, yet I know that I wouldn't want to be kept on life-support systems if there were no hope. Her complete trust in us will make this decision even more difficult, and I pray that she will go quietly in her sleep.

When quail hunting season began in 1998, I planned to leave Cokie at home because of her blindness. I tried to slip away, but the smell of my boots and the smell of other dogs and horses on my hunting clothes betrayed me. Cokie began to sulk, and I believe she was becoming depressed. I couldn't enjoy hunting without her, knowing how much it meant to her, so I relented and took her along to ride in the dog truck. She sat with her head sticking out the window, enjoying being a part of the hunt. Cokie was born to retrieve, so several times during the hunt when we were in a place where Cokie couldn't hurt herself, I dropped dead quail for her to find. I lifted her out of the truck, gave her the "hunt dead" command she wanted to hear, and let her do her thing. Her nose was still keen, and it didn't take long for her to find the bird and bring it to me. Just being with me and being useful was all she wanted. I can identify with that. Finding meaning for our lives, knowing we belong somewhere, and using the God-given gifts for those we love are the secrets of happiness.

Bill's beloved Cokie inspires him to love fully and unconditionally.

Cokie has taught us much about love. She has taught us that to fully love, to love unconditionally, we must accept the pain and the liability that go with it, that we must be willing to totally let go of the object of our love because love is never possessive. We could have avoided the pain we are feeling as we contemplate her death by not letting Cokie come into our lives. But we would have missed a tremendous amount of joy and love for her, each other, and others had we refused this gift of God. I believe that God created dogs with short lives so that we humans could learn this lesson. His gift of love is what enables us to become His willing servants.

I have also been blessed with great friends. There were seven of us who began elementary school together: Gene Dykes, Jack King, Bubber Scruggs, Joe Flowers, Frank Foley, David Lewis, and me. Sue Marie dubbed us the "Magnificent Seven" because we were so close. We were an earlier, nicer version of Frank Sinatra's "Rat Pack." Sue Marie claims we were quite a challenge to the wives, and there's no doubt we all married women way beyond our potential.

No matter what was going on in our lives, we always found time to play golf and tennis, fish, and hunt together. Later, Cliff Averett, Ben Tyler, Brother Knight, and Tom Molloy qualified to join our group, and we had some great experiences together. We loved to go to the Florida Everglades, one of the last wilderness areas in the country. We would board a houseboat at Everglade City and go deep into the creeks and the 10,000 islands that make up the Everglades. We would venture out in a small boat to fish for snook and tarpon all day and return to the houseboat at night. We often went days without seeing a sign of another human being.

On what turned out to be our last trip down there, Tom Molloy and I were returning to the houseboat just before dark after fishing a tidal creek. Our "experienced" guide, and I use that term sarcastically, hit a cypress stump, and Tom and I were thrown overboard. The boat's propeller hit my foot, nearly severing it. We were in water where a huge shark had taken a tarpon off my line the night before, so I was in a special hurry to get back in the boat. We also had another problem. Tom couldn't swim, so I swam over to him, and we bobbed up and down back to the boat. When I got in the boat, I discovered the condition of my foot. Tom held a cushion over the wound and I found a pressure point that slowed down the bleeding. When we got to the houseboat, Cliff and David jumped into the boat with me, and we took off in the dark to find Everglade City, a trek that took about an hour. When we arrived at the hospital, an orthopedic surgeon wheeled me into the operating room and went to work. I found out later that he had trained under Jack Hughston at what is now the Hughston Sports Medicine Hospital in Columbus. As soon as my foot healed, I was able to resume tennis and other activities without any handicap, although I could fake a limp if someone hit one past me on the tennis court.

Another of my close friends from kindergarten was Steve Knight, who lived across the street from me. When we were little, we used to communicate with each other with our bugles. One toot meant "Can you come over?" Two toots in response meant "yes," and three meant "no." This system worked very well for us until one morning after an attack of diarrhea, I gave too forceful a toot on my bugle. My mother suggested that the telephone might be a better way to communicate, and my sisters' teasing every time I pulled my bugle out convinced me she was right.

When Steve returned from the war, a dentist friend made him a set of false teeth that protruded in every direction. When our other friends returned home from the service, I took them over to visit Steve, warning them that he had experienced a horrible accident while in the Army that had left his mouth terribly disfigured. I told them that he was very sensitive about the way he looked and please not to ask him about it or stare at his mouth. What happened was exactly what we had anticipated. There was much staring at hands and feet, much looking out the window and at the ceiling, and many stolen glances at his mouth. I, of course, had to keep a straight face through Steve's performance. Steve, Paul Berry, and I were the organizers of the "Little Theatre Group" I wrote about earlier, and "The Teeth" was our last performance. It was nice to have a repeat of the performances we had before we all went off to war. Steve went on from our foolishness together to become a great public servant, serving as a state senator, city and county commissioner, and mayor of Columbus.

Looking back, I can see how much "seriousness" has pushed "foolishness" out of my life, and it gives me a new resolve to let my "child" play occasionally. Even Jesus said we must come as a child. Although I'm not sure that this is what he meant, I don't think it hurts to make a fool of myself every now and then, if I don't do it too often. It does me good to see the heads of our companies—Steve Butler, Brad Turner,

Tim Horne, and Mat Swift—do crazy things like letting other team members hit them in the face with a pie as part of our celebrations of success. We should always take our work and responsibilities seriously, but never ourselves.

The husbands of Sue Marie's friends were added to my list of companions later on, and for years I played tennis with my cousin Hooper Turner, Hank Wiley, Charlie Flowers, and John Kinnett.

The great thing about real friends is that you can go for days, even years, without seeing them, and when you get together again, you can pick up right where you left off. I was always grateful for this because as I grew older, family and other things cut in on the time I could spend with friends. More and more, I appreciate the value of being connected with others in solid relationships.

Thoughts While Passing Through

- No man has freedom until who he is coincides with what he does. I think that's what God meant when He said that His name is "I am." John fully understood this when he said, "God is love." Love is both a noun and verb.
- There's a vast difference between saying "I love you because I need you" and saying "I need you because I love you."
- Marriages don't die overnight. They die slowly if they are not nurtured daily with love and affirmation and communication.
- The greatest joy parents have is watching their children become great parents. It's also fun to watch them deal with some of the problems we had to deal with when our children were growing up.
- Unconditional love means loving a person the way they need loving, not the way they want to be loved.
- I hope that I will be loved for what I am rather than for what I pretend to be.
- Is there any difference between believing there is no God and living as if there is no God?
- When you pretend, you stay the same. When you're real, you change.

CHAPTER 5

DOING THE RIGHT THING

I was chosen to lead my company before I could even talk, and that probably was just as well. My grandfather was a remarkable man in many ways. He was the founder of Columbus Bank and Trust Company (with G. Gunby Jordan), which is now Synovus Financial Corporation, and the W. C. Bradley Company. He was also one of the initial developers of the modern-day Coca-Cola Company. No doubt he was a keen judge of business opportunities, but I seriously question his judgment of people, at least in my own case. The only criteria my grandfather used in selecting me was that I was the only male heir in the family.

When I came back from the war, I was ready to learn about the companies that made up our holdings so I would be ready when the time came for me to take over. At that time we owned the Columbus Iron Works, the Columbus Grocery Company, the W. C. Bradley Company, Columbus Bank and Trust Company, and the Eagle and Phenix Mills.

The only training I received about leadership was observing my grandfather and my dad as they ran our companies. The good news was that I had lots of years to observe them both, and the bad news was that I didn't see them doing anything except walking around and listening to others. They did do two things that impressed me, however.

During the years of the Great Depression in the 1930s my grandfather kept the Eagle and Phenix mills running, though textile mills all over the country were shutting their doors and leaving their employees jobless and hungry. During that time our company couldn't sell the goods it manufactured, and it piled up huge inventories. In fact, the mill ran out of money and issued script to the employees so they could buy groceries for their families. Then, when the depression was over, my grandfather had all those goods in the warehouses and sold them when demand picked up, and it worked out okay. But he came awfully close to bankrupting himself because of that.

Second, in the early 1940s my grandfather and my dad formed a foundation with 10% of the Bradley Company stock, which at that time was valued at $400,000. This stock today is valued at well over $350 million, and we give away 5% of the market value of the stock every year.

In those first years about the only thing I had going for me was that I had a little practical experience working in the companies. During my high school and college years I had worked in many of the departments of both CB&T and the W. C. Bradley Company, and I had many bosses who were ready, willing, and able to tell me what I should be doing. For two summers I worked in the Iron Works in the foundry helping the fastest molder they had. We were right next to the cupola, which is the hottest, dirtiest place in the foundry. I made a lot of friends and developed a mutual respect among the people who worked there. And what good advice I got, I got from those folks. The experience convinced me that going to college was a good thing.

There were a lot of very capable managers to learn from at all of my grandfather's companies: Henry Burrus at the W. C. Bradley Company, Elliott Waddell and Toombs Howard at Columbus Iron Works, Claude Brown at Columbus Grocery and Supply Company, Jack Pease at CB&T, Frank Bradley at Eagle and Phenix Mills, and Forbes Bradley at Columbus Manufacturing Company. Forbes and Frank were kin, the last two of my grandfather's nephews. All of those managers had survived the Depression, and most were approaching retirement age at a time when business conditions were changing rapidly.

After I started working full-time for the company, I simply didn't know what my job was. I just hung around our corporate offices in the W. C. Bradley Company warehouse with my dad, asking him questions about how to run things, what to do. I didn't get answers that I felt like I could take and say "Fine, I'll take that and go with it and do something about it."

My friend, Jack King, was in the same boat. He was an Army officer and had come home to work in his family's business, King Grocery Company. He was given the job of pushing the soft drink cart, what they called the "dope wagon," at the Eagle and Phenix mill. I didn't have anything to do, so I'd go down there and help him load the wagon. We would bemoan our fate and how we, who had been leaders of men who had saved the world, didn't have a job that meant anything and didn't know what was going on.

What I discovered surprised me. I think one of the great things you learn by going to college is that there is a lot you don't know. But people who haven't been to college think you know everything. So that was kind of my dad's attitude. He didn't go to college, and he felt that since I had graduated from Georgia Tech with a degree in business management, I should have all the answers. He pretty much turned the leadership of the companies over to me as soon as he could.

My dad got into the business because my grandfather wanted him to. He had a good job with Columbus Power Company (now Georgia Power Company), and he was happy there. But my grandfather didn't have a son and needed somebody to take over, and my dad was valuable in a lot of ways. I know he worked harder than anybody I've ever seen. He thought he ought to be the first one at work in the morning and the last one to leave at night. In fact, after I started working at the company, I began coming in earlier than he did, so he started coming in earlier than I did. This went on for several weeks, and I finally said "Now wait a minute. This has got to stop. I'm not going to get up at 6 o'clock and go to work."

When my grandfather died in 1947, a more definitive job opened up for me. I began working with my dad in partnership to run the companies, the bank, and other things. Together we made some significant changes. We appealed to Mills Lane, Chief Executive Officer of C&S

Bank in Atlanta, to help us find a president for CB&T. He put us in touch with James Blanchard, Jimmy Blanchard's father. With the help of a lot of people, we started reorganizing the businesses and brought in some new people who were good managers.

At age 32 I was running our companies, and they were profitable by past standards. But, my impression was that all the businesses were slowly dying. There is a saying about how you shouldn't waste your energy swimming against the current. Don't try to swim up the river; go with the flow. Our companies at that time were going against the flow, and we were falling behind.

In the case of the Columbus Iron Works, its two biggest products were becoming obsolete. Potbellied stoves were going out of style because of gas heaters. Of course, we could have gone into the gas heater business, but central heating was taking over there. And with the farm implements, I guess we could have tackled John Deere and McCormick and those large manufacturers, but that didn't look like a very good strategy. We were just trying to find a niche where nobody was and a demand that nobody was meeting. We brainstormed about what we could do to replace the potbellied stove. Realizing that people had more leisure time than ever before and that they might want to spend it outdoors, we came up with the charcoal grill idea in 1949. When we first started manufacturing the charcoal grills, we had a salesman named Tommy Tucker who would dress up in a red chef's outfit, set up our grill in a strip shopping center, and cook a ham over charcoals. The sound of ham sizzling on the grill and the wonderful aroma drifting over the shopping center would draw a crowd, and he'd cut off slices and give them to people.

Later I saw a gas grill somewhere and told Manning Culpepper, who was in charge of sales at that time, that it was something we ought to investigate and pursue. Of course, that is the bulk of our business now—the Char-Broil gas grill. Since then we've acquired a number of companies, including Thermos, Oklahoma Joe's, and the New Braunfels Smoker Company, and now have the lion's share of the grill business. In the early years if we made 250 grills a day, we thought we'd had a big day. In 1999 we make 17,000 a day.

Char-Broil, the world's largest manufacturer of outdoor grills, boasts a 2,000,000 square-foot facility in north Columbus.

In the case of the Columbus Grocery Company, the day of the "mom and pop" grocery store was just about over because the big chain stores like A&P, Kroger, and Winn-Dixie were taking over. They offered customers a wider range of merchandise and because they dealt in volume, they could offer better prices. The corner grocery stores and those in rural areas were going out of business, and they were the ones who bought our products. Closing down our grocery operation was a tough decision because it was still limping along and making a profit. As a leader, I think you just have to realize that things are going to change and be sensitive to those things.

Running the businesses turned out to be quite an undertaking, and I realized pretty early that I needed help, that there were skills I didn't possess. Something I think all managers need to do is to make a good assessment of their strengths and weaknesses. My strengths were problem solving and people skills. I was not a detail person who liked to sit down and look at numbers. I needed somebody who could do that, and I brought Otis LeMay into our company and made him chief financial officer and then made him president in a short time because he had those skills I didn't. A former Internal Revenue Service agent and the head of his own accounting firm, his skills were invaluable to us because many of our problems were tax-related.

Knowing that the world was changing and that if we wanted to continue in business we'd have to change with it, we started looking for other products with growth potential. Needless to say, we had several false starts. One time we went into the forge business, making parts for agricultural implements. That was not a good business to be in, but I didn't know it at the time. We were dependent on other people to sell the product; all we were doing was selling parts to them. We found that when the agricultural economy slowed down, we were the first ones cut off.

Another time we started manufacturing low-cost modular homes, which sounded like a great idea after a lot of research, but it just didn't work. There were people—I know of two or three—who had their hearts so much in the modular home business that they couldn't stand the failure of it, having to back off and be wrong. But we got to the point where it was pretty obvious we couldn't make it. Many larger companies, like Boise Cascade, also tried and failed at the modular home business. When we started it, though, we were excited about it and built a plant in the Bradley Industrial Park to manufacture the components. The good thing about that venture was that when one of the large discount stores started ordering large numbers of our grills, we were able to move our grill manufacturing business from downtown into that plant.

In addition to revamping our company, my dad and I remained active as directors of CB&T. James Blanchard Sr. gave us great leadership at CB&T until his untimely death left us without a CEO. We were at a loss as to what to do, so we appealed to Trust Company of Georgia to allow Bill Curry, retired chief executive officer of its Columbus bank, to serve as CEO on an interim basis. I think the relationship between my dad and grandfather and C&S and Trust Company is significant. Though some saw us as competitors, they came to our assistance. A permanent solution to our CEO problem occurred in a remarkable way. Many people liked to claim credit for the hiring of Jimmy Blanchard, and I believe I'm the only one of those still living. Jimmy was a young attorney with no banking experience, but we convinced him to apprentice with Bill Curry and become our CEO. With that, Jimmy and CB&T were ready to begin an exciting era of growth and expansion.

We created a bank holding company, called CB&T Bancshares, to look at acquisitions in Georgia. My dad was chairman of the board for many years. CB&T Bancshares prospered, and in 1989, we changed its name to Synovus Financial Corporation as we expanded into other southeastern states. In 1983 CB&T launched Total System Services Inc. from its backroom data processing department, and it has become one of the world's largest credit, debit, commercial, and private label card processing companies. Our banking operations have been successful beyond our expectations, not only financially, but also through their people development emphasis.

My dad and I also continued my grandfather's involvement with the Coca-Cola Company. Dad sat on the Coca-Cola board from 1923 to 1980, and I was elected to the board in 1980 and served for 16 years until my retirement in 1996. Being on this board was very beneficial for me and for the company because I learned much from that group that I could bring back and apply here, including ways to share profits, motivate and train people, manage human resources, and market products.

Bill Turner (top right) was a diligent and committed member of the Coca-Cola Company board of directors for 16 years.

I was on the board at an exciting time in Coke's history. When I joined the Coke board, the average age of its members was about 75, a management change was long overdue, and competition with Pepsi was fierce. Gradually, some of the older members retired, allowing new blood to come onto the board. When it came time to pass the torch, the former chairman made an announcement that he had five vice-chairmen and his successor would be one of these guys. It created a horribly competitive set-up. But when Roberto Goizueta was named chairman—he was one of the five, but not the favorite to be picked—things settled down. He and Don Keough had agreed that if one of them was picked as chief executive officer, he would pick the other as chief operating officer. Don was a marketing man, and Roberto was a strategist and organizer. They made a great team.

I was also on the board when the company introduced a product called New Coke. Pepsi was conducting a very successful "best by taste" test marketing campaign at the time. The board, after conducting taste tests of New Coke, approved management's decision to put it on the market. Not long after, we also approved management's decision to take it off. The phones just rang off the hooks with people protesting taking the old Coke off the market. It shook up the market and developed a loyalty that hadn't existed before. It was really the greatest marketing coup there has ever been. I saw Roberto make many great decisions to move the company forward, but his decision to remove New Coke from the market is the one that impressed me most and gave me the most confidence in his ability to lead because he recognized the mistake and acted quickly to correct it.

I missed an opportunity when I was on the Coke board to really get to know Roberto. What I saw going up to Atlanta for two-day meetings was a brilliant businessman. And yet I've realized since his death that Roberto in a lot of ways in his personal life was a lot like me—a family man who saw his job as a mission and who believed in giving back to the community. He put $85 million in his own foundation to benefit others. He had a book on his desk all the time called *Business as a Calling*. I think the reason I didn't get to know him better was that I always felt like an oddball at the Coca-Cola Company because everybody up there was always dropping big names of business tycoons and talking about finances; I just didn't want to get caught up in that game. That was not me. But I missed an opportunity to really get to know him, and I regret it. We miss that opportunity a lot with people by not letting our faces show through.

During the time I was on the board, Coke's stock value increased 41 times. I've always been intrigued by my grandfather's decision to invest in Coke and to encourage others to invest in it. He must have had a strong belief in Coca-Cola. It has always amazed me. I know of a schoolteacher who bought some Coke stock at his insistence, and she left something like $3 million to her church just from that investment. I can understand if you have plenty of money where you'd be comfortable taking a flyer on something; if you lose it, so what. But to encourage others to invest their life savings took a lot of guts!

Not only was my grandfather a believer in Coke, but his friends were, too. One of my grandfather's friends was a Quincy, Florida, banker named Pat Monroe. When people would come into the bank to borrow money, he'd offer to loan them a little bit extra to buy Coca-Cola stock. Today Quincy has the highest per capita ownership of Coca-Cola of any place in the country. Mr. Pat had a huge family, some 20 children, and I was fraternity brothers with three of his sons at Georgia Tech. CB&T later acquired Mr. Pat's bank.

As our companies were undergoing changes, I began my own personal metamorphosis as well. Early in my career I realized that getting up every morning just to make a buck was not something that thrilled me to death and that if I didn't do something, it was going to be a pretty miserable existence. I didn't need to work for money. I already had most of the things that people seek in life. Something was missing, and I wanted to know what it was. I sat down at that time and wrote what it would take to give meaning to my job, what it would take to make me get up in the morning excited about going to work.

I thought long and hard about it, and I decided that my goal would have to be to create an atmosphere where people, including me, would grow—materially, intellectually, and spiritually. Seeing people grow was the thing that was important. I felt that if I needed meaning in my life, most everybody else would need it, too. In order for people to feel good about working for the company, we'd have to share a common vision of what the company was going to be. I knew I would have to meet the needs of the people who were working there to help them grow. This is something I kept as a priority as I assumed more responsibility in the company.

Through the years I have held a number of leadership positions in our companies. I've been chief executive officer of the W. C. Bradley Company, chairman of CB&T, chairman of Synovus Financial Corporation, and chairman of the executive committee of Synovus. As my leadership roles changed, my thoughts on leadership matured. Some of the things I thought were important as a young leader turned out not to be so important after all. But there are some key elements that remained constant, and I believe them to be truths worth passing on.

In 1965, as part of a group exercise, I shared my goals at a workshop for W. C. Bradley Company managers. I include these early notes to show my thoughts at the time since they were the foundation for much of my thinking later and for many of the projects that the company and the Foundation undertook. They are not a blueprint for others to follow because each leader must find his/her own way. They are simply food for thought.

> This is an attempt to put in written form my own values and goals—both personal and for the W. C. Bradley Company. These thoughts are based to a large extent on my own personal philosophy that (1) happiness and satisfaction come from working to achieve some acceptable goal and from finding meaning and purpose for our existence; and (2) until a person establishes some sort of priority system on his values and goals, he will be neither productive nor happy because he will be pulled in first one direction and then another as each of the values struggle for the position of authority in his life. In fact, I believe happiness and success can be measured in exact proportion to a person's ability to define relative values.
>
> Like anyone else, my personal philosophy is the result of a combination of living, study, observation of others, and prayerful meditation. By the process of elimination, by trial and error, I have come to the strong conviction that happiness does not come from success, it does not come from material possessions, it does not come from being well liked or admired or even being loved—though I

know all of these things are an important part of living. Happiness comes in only one way: from working, even struggling, to achieve meaningful and acceptable goals and with it a reason for being. If this is true, it behooves us all not to set for ourselves goals that are too easily attainable, for in reaching these goals we lose our happiness, unless we have already set our sights on even more distant and more worthy goals. (An aside, written in 1986) I believe now that direction is more important than goals.

For example, a child finds happiness in anticipation of having a bicycle, only to find that it did not fulfill his needs as he thought it would. A man works hard to provide his family with a house, a new car, social position, or recognition—only these things are not what they're cracked up to be. A mother who devotes her life to working for her children wakes up one day to find that they are gone, and she feels she is no longer needed and that her life has lost its meaning. A good part of the patient population at the Bradley Center is composed of people with this problem, and we have found that where we can help these people find a new reason for living and a new meaning to life, we can greatly improve their mental health. My eight-year-old son expressed to me his own need to work to achieve goals when he said, "A little boy thinks he wants something real bad until he gets it" and "It's lots more fun to work at building something than it is to play in it."

What has this got to do with the W. C. Bradley Company?

It is my belief that a businessman must view his business not as something set apart from the other areas of his life with a different value system than we would find in family, social, or religious life, but as a part of the whole and a means toward an end. It is only when we view life as a whole with all elements related and interrelated that the larger possibilities of life are revealed. It is my belief that the early founders of this country, guided by strong religious convictions, viewed life in this way and that many of the problems we face today are caused by our tendency to separate and compartmentalize each phase of our life with a different code of ethics and a different value system. Such an approach to life leaves voids and vacuums that something will fill. The growth of unions, growing centralized federal government, socialism, and many other problems are direct results of our failure to meet our responsibilities as businessmen that we gladly accept in other areas of our lives. I believe that a large part of communism's success and appeal comes from relating all of a man's activities to a central and meaningful goal. If I am correct on this thesis, then for me or any other working person to find real satisfaction in work, we must set business goals that go beyond making an ever-increasing profit or earning an ever-increasing salary. And these goals must be compatible in every way with the goals in other areas of life. In fact, the goals and value system must be the same.

My Central Goal: To respond with my best effort to God's will for my life as He reveals it to me. Through study, prayer, and meditation, seek to discover God's will and to move closer to Him
• To set an example as a Christian businessman for others to follow
• To pay the rent for the space I occupy
• To leave the world better than I found it

I. Church
A place to worship, a place to recharge spiritual batteries, a place to get a clearer focus on objectives, a place to take inventory, a place to learn and share, a place to renew faith by sharing experiences with others

II. Family
Objectives
• To provide opportunities for growth—spiritual, intellectual, physical, and material
• To teach the meaning of love and discipline
• To help them develop their own orderly value system
• To prepare for life; to give as well as to take
• To help each member be a better person who lives life on a higher plane than I do
• To provide for their well-being, but not to rob them of a sense of accomplishment
III. Business—A means of reaching other objectives
A. Central Goal
To demonstrate that the free enterprise system is the best social and economic system devised by man. Profit and growth, while not the end goals of business, are the essential ingredients in attaining all other goals.

B. To meet and exceed our responsibilities to:
　1. Stockholders—to provide a return on investment as good as they can get anywhere else
　2. Employees
　　a. To create an atmosphere for growth—spiritual, intellectual, professional, and material
　　b. To reward according to contribution to company goals
　　c. To provide sense of meaning to each job
　3. Customers—best quality and service at best price
　4. Society—community, state, and nation
　　a. To provide financial support to religious, charitable, educational, and civic endeavors—corporate and individual
　　b. To cultivate an interest in politics and participation in government
　　c. To contribute to my community and church
　　d. To provide greater employment opportunity
　　e. To train and help develop more responsible citizens
C. How—Each division head will be responsible for developing the division's own program to accomplish these objectives by:
　1. Planning for a growth rate (to be defined by each division) at a minimum of 10% per year (inflation 4%) to be stepped up to 15% in two years
　2. Training—informal and formal
　　a. See that each employee develops his own training program
　　b. See that each employee develops those under him as both a manager and as a well-rounded responsible citizen
　　c. Teach by example; attitudes beget attitudes
　　d. Develop a formal program of company publications, discussion groups, educational television, seminars, and short courses
　3. Improve communications by understanding values of others and seeing that others understand your values, but not by imposing your values on others
D. Summary—Our company will have accomplished its objective when a sweeper at Columbus Iron Works, the W. C. Bradley Company, Columbus Grocery and Supply Company, or any other division feels he is not merely pushing dirt across a floor but is playing a real part in building a better world.

1. I will ask each division head who reports to me to give me in detail his plans for his division.
2. I also ask that each person reporting to me name those under him who could succeed him when they are ready and what he is doing to implement their development. I feel that no person is worthy of promotion unless he has trained someone to take his place.
3. I will also ask that those who report to me follow this same procedure with those who report to them.

Building on these goals and refining them made me think about what it means to be a leader. I believe that leadership can be found on the loading dock or behind the secretary's desk, as well as in the executive office.

I don't know if leadership can be taught, but I know it can be discovered and developed. I am not talking about management. You can be a good manager without being a leader. A manager must have authority commensurate with his responsibility, whereas a leader will find ways to influence others without authority or title. Mr. Robert Woodruff was largely responsible for the development of Coca-Cola and the city of Atlanta for well over 20 years, a good part of the time without having the title of chairman or president of the Coca-Cola Company. He was known, however, to everyone as "The Boss."

Many people would say, "Anyone could make the kind of mark that Mr. Woodruff made, considering his financial resources." But it should be clearly understood that money was a byproduct of his leadership. He began as a truck salesman for the White Motor Company.

I believe there are three kinds of leaders. The first type is the transformational leader. He has a passion for a purpose and has a power of commitment toward that purpose. He believes so strongly in a cause that he draws others to him. Mahatma Gandhi, Dr. Martin Luther King, Bishop Arthur Moore, and Bill Bright of Campus Crusade for Christ are examples of this kind of leadership. The second type of leader is the transactional leader who has the ability to listen, assimilate, collate, negotiate, translate, and activate the aspirations of a group into a plan. Ronald Reagan is a good example of this type of leader. The third type of leader is a servant leader who meets the needs of others as they accomplish particular tasks, grows other servant leaders, and builds a common vision. Jesus Christ and Mother Theresa are models of this leadership type. Ideally, the great leaders blend all three of these styles.

The chief concern of a leader should be the vision. "Where there is no vision, the people perish" (Prov 29:18). The vision must have meaning because man cannot live without meaning. The vision must be holistic and congruent, encompassing the church, the family, the community, and the institution. If it doesn't, values and priorities will conflict. In addition to the work center, the community and the family environments must be protected. The vision must have passion because passion is contagious. The leader must see that the vision has all these things and must be owned and communicated by all. If the vision is owned and if communication is good, there is no need for an organizational chart. The organization will take care of itself.

My favorite philosopher, Yogi Berra said, "You can observe a lot just by watching." I have been in a unique position, through no fault of my own, to observe many outstanding leaders. They were all different, but they had similar qualities that I believe are necessary if one wants to be a successful leader.

(1) A leader knows himself. Robert Louis Stevenson said, "To be what we are and to become what we are capable of becoming is the only end of life." A leader makes an honest assessment of his strengths and weaknesses and concentrates his efforts on the areas where he is strongest, while not ignoring the areas where he is weak. He either develops himself or delegates to others responsibilities in his area of weakness. A leader doesn't waste energy comparing himself with others or trying to emulate others; he realizes that he is a unique, one-of-a-kind individual. I love the statement that the little boy made, "I'm not much on my 9s, but I am a hound dog on my 7s."

(2) A leader has self-worth and believes the world is better because he is living in it. Self-worth is what gives a leader a strong sense of personal mastery that compels him to take charge, direct affairs, and influence others' thoughts and actions. A leader has a healthy ego that is comfortable with the loneliness that leadership requires. A strong sense of self-worth is also what allows a leader to admit failure and

allows those around him to be free to fail. A leader is strong enough that he doesn't need the approval of others in decision making. He does not make decisions on the basis of wanting to be loved. A leader wants those around him to experience this same self-worth.

(3) A leader has creativity and problem-solving ability and understands that the business of business is discovery, innovation, and creativity and that these processes lead to dramatic breakthroughs.

(4) A leader feels a mission to profoundly alter human relationships. He cares about people and their needs and encourages people to be the best they can be. In one of his books Jimmy Carter tells about an interview he had as a young naval officer with Admiral Rickover. During this interview Admiral Rickover demonstrated greater knowledge than Carter on every subject discussed and terminated the interview by asking, "Where did you finish in your class at Annapolis?" Carter responded with great pride, "I finished number 50 in a class of 800." Admiral Rickover then looked at him with his steely blue eyes and asked, "Did you do your best?" When Carter responded, "Well, no, I guess not," Admiral Rickover, after two minutes of silence, said, "Why not?" and returned to his work. The issue before a leader and those he leads is not what he can be but what he is willing to become. A leader measures every day, not only in terms of profit, but also in how much better we have all become. A minister friend of mine asks his congregation each month to make a list of what they plan to do to make themselves better, to make their church better, to make their families better, and to make their community better.

(5) A leader is driven by principles that give meaning and purpose to life, and he wants meaning for the lives around him. A leader has clear values and goals. He can usually pull a piece of paper from his desk that lists simply his values and goals.

(6) A leader has control of his time and develops a personal rhythm in his life. He knows how much rest he needs, how much study he needs, how much recreation he needs, how much exercise he needs, and how much prayer he needs to keep his cup filled to overflowing for others. A leader budgets his time well in advance for priority things. My Dad would let nothing interfere with his fishing on Thursday afternoon, and woe be unto the person who tried to schedule a meeting on

the Sabbath. It is axiomatic that the things most essential—family, recreation, study, exercise, and spiritual renewal—don't cry out if we neglect them but will take their toll over time when neglected. It is also axiomatic that unseized time flows to weaknesses. We often spend most of our time on things that we do second best and neglect those things that we do best.

(7) A leader is flexible and recognizes that the rate of change inside an organization must exceed external change if the organization is to lead. A leader also recognizes the long-term advantages found in human resources and that he must lead others by example to change.

(8) A leader models what he wants to see happen. This is a simple statement, but it is a profound one.

(9) A leader creates an atmosphere for growth and feels an obligation to create a culture that has pride, confidence, fairness, service, and creativity at the heart of its philosophy. Most people hate work but love accomplishment. The goal of the leader is cooperation, not coercion. Communication is essential to creating such a culture. To see that the communication channels are clear, a leader must learn to listen and to listen "between the lines," not only to hear what is said, but also to hear what is not said. Someone said that great leaders comprehend more in a look, in a word, in a touch than most do in long conversation.

(10) A leader understands the use of power and knows that it can corrupt. Friedrich Nietzsche said, "Those who don't want power are the only ones fit to hold it." And I believe it was Nietzsche who said, "In fighting a dragon, we must be careful not to become the dragon."

(11) A leader is a steward. I love the example that John the Baptist set when the crowd was leaving him to follow Jesus. He said, "A man receives nothing unless it is given to him from heaven" and then he followed by saying, "He [Jesus] must grow greater and I less and less." This is the philosophy of servant leadership. A true leader builds everyone up except himself, and his goal is to grow less and less as others grow more and more.

(12) A leader has spiritual strength. Arnold Toynbee said that the spiritual strength of leaders is a matter of life and death for any society and that a society lives or dies according to how it meets the challenge

of its time. Spiritual strength is what enables a leader to stand firm when failure, pressure, coercion, ridicule, abuse, and temptation come his way. President Lyndon Johnson once stated, "There are times when a leader must stand like a jackass in a hailstorm and take it." The leader then moves on again toward his vision. Spiritual strength is what makes a leader view himself as a servant and a steward of the resources under his control.

My father, though he didn't know it, was a servant leader. I succeeded my father several times in a variety of responsibilities, and each time my appreciation for him grew because of the conditions he left. I appreciated the energy and enthusiasm he brought to every task. I appreciated the integrity and values that he instilled in everyone around him. I appreciated his keen sense of responsibility and concern for others. I appreciated the atmosphere of creativity he generated. I appreciated the financial, moral, and spiritual strength that the W. C. Bradley Company had because of him. But most of all, I appreciated the quality of people he attracted around him.

A friend of mine sent me a clipping on leadership that reads, "A leader is best when people barely know that he exists, not so good when people obey and acclaim him, bad when people fear him, and worse when they despise him. But of a good leader who talks little when his work is done and his aim fulfilled, they will say, 'We did it ourselves.' "

Part of our commitment in our companies is to put people first in the value chain, but someone who doesn't know and understand our companies would think that the reason we put people first is for the purpose of generating exceptional profit. That is not the case. That would be manipulative. Exceptional profit is a byproduct of exceptional people caring. There have been times in our history when profit was not there, but that did not stop us from putting people first. To keep our people employed, we continued to operate unprofitable businesses until we could make changes.

I have never considered myself to be a good manager, but I am good at caring for people. At times I hope too much rather than face reality. This has caused me to stay too long with people who were not performing. Rather than being surgical, I have delayed in taking decisive action, with the result, as one manager put it, of "cutting the puppy dog's tail off an inch at a time." This has caused grief for the people involved. Sometimes I have not read financial numbers realistically. To me, governing by the numbers was like trying to drive a car by looking in the rear view mirror. I would much prefer to look ahead, even though I couldn't see what was out there. I do believe that people know I care, and this has fostered creativity and freedom and has attracted and held the good managers who can steer the ship far better than I.

But I'm not just talking about putting people first; I'm talking about love, and love is a gift from God available to all of us and has been claimed by many within our company. This is what Jesus meant when he said, "You are the light of the world" (Matt 5:14). This is what he meant when he said, "The kingdom of heaven is like leaven" (Matt 13:33). One loving spirit can set a soul aflame, and this is why our companies are special.

Many things have happened, some large and others small, that reinforce and affirm this belief. One day as I was walking with my dog on the Riverwalk, I saw a young woman who works with us. She was sitting on a bench, going over her prayer list, and she said, "Mr. T., it's so great to work for a company where it's okay to pray for each other and where we are asked to pray for our company." Also, one of our team members asked and received permission from our CEO to have an e-mail devotional on our computers each morning. Different team members prepare the devotional every day. I also received a note from a boy who comes to my Sunday School class occasionally. I really wouldn't have thought that he had gained anything from our lessons, but he wrote, "Thanks for being a walking reminder of the true purpose behind our earthly lives: that is, to love and care for other people, and this love is not possible without Jesus in one's heart."

That's how we make disciples, not by beating them over the head with the Bible, not by shaming them or scaring them or making them feel guilty. As we go, Jesus' light will shine through, and others will see what's missing in their lives, and then they will want to become disciples. That's what has happened in our companies because so many have become light and leaven. That's what can happen in our families and our world.

While I was discovering my own leadership style at the company, I was also learning about my community through civic involvement. In addition to belonging on numerous boards and working on race relations in the community, I was named to the committee that worked on the consolidation of the city and county governments in the 1960s. It's one of the committees I'm proudest of having served on. Each council member appointed one representative, and I was approved for the at-large position. Mayor J. R. Allen was an unusual leader, a great leader. He was a young man who had come up through the cotton mills, and yet he was a successful businessman and had the confidence of this town. And he had vision. He is probably the one who encouraged consolidation more than anybody else. Columbus was totally divided about the issue.

We were on many issues a community divided. I can remember somebody in the state government saying, "Why would we do anything for Columbus? We'd make half the people mad and half the people happy. We'll go somewhere else and get a better payoff on the money we spend." I think that's the primary reason we got left off the interstate, the fact that Columbus didn't have a cohesive group working together to make things happen.

Although I enjoyed being CEO of our company, the time came when I felt it was time for me to step down. Anyone who knows me well knows that I have a big ego and that I enjoyed the prestige of being chief executive officer of the W. C. Bradley Company. The decision to retire was hard for me. But it was made easier because I was handing the reins over to two people whom I dearly love, two people I watched and hopefully helped grow from infancy. My dad used to say that each new generation should be an improvement over their parents', and this is certainly true with Steve Butler, my son Brad, and all of my children.

What follows are the remarks I made at our stockholders meeting when I resigned as chairman of our company. I include these because I know that I couldn't have retired gracefully if it hadn't been for God's grace.

August 4, 1987

As you know, the main purpose of this meeting is the changing of the guard. This is the time when I step down as chairman and Lovick Corn steps down as vice-chairman of our company. I will appoint Neal Gregory as temporary chairman while I make three simultaneous motions.

(1) I move that the board accept my resignation as chairman and Lovick's resignation as vice-chairman and also our resignations as officers in any subsidiary companies related to W. C. Bradley Company. Of course, we will remain as board members on all boards.

(2) I move that Steve Butler be elected as chairman and chief executive officer of the W. C. Bradley Company and Brad Turner be elected president and chief operating officer of the W. C. Bradley Company.

(3) I move that I be elected chairman and Lovick be elected vice-chairman of the executive committee of the company.

Before I ask you to vote on these motions, I would like to explain the reasoning behind them.

I have always considered it to be one of the prime responsibilities of leadership to create an atmosphere of growth. When you do this properly, people grow, and you need to stay out of their way. Steve and Brad are ready to assume these offices in our company. They have served their apprenticeship in a variety of ways. For the past several years they have experienced a trial by fire and have handled it well. They have gone through the tedious and sometimes painful process of strategically planning for the future of the company. They are well on the way to transforming the company. Programs and people are in place to do this, and I've never been more excited about our future. I wouldn't step down if I didn't fully believe this.

I have always believed that people who want power aren't fit to hold it, but when you push power away, there is no limit to the power you will have. Jim Blanchard tells about the head of a large New York advertising agency who gives his new managers a Russian doll with a successively smaller doll inside each doll as you open it. Along with the doll he gives his managers a note that reads: "If you hire people who are smaller than you are and stifle their growth, you will soon be managing a company of dwarfs. But if you hire people who are bigger than you are and encourage their growth, you will soon be managing a company of giants." Steve and Brad are prepared to manage a company of giants.

I want to explain my new role. I am not retiring. I have devoted my entire life to this company, and I don't think that I could ever fully retire. My grandfather wrote me a note on my eighth birthday telling me that he expected me to lead our company, and I took him seriously.

I will be in my office every day. Steve and I have worked out a system to keep me fully informed, and I will be available as a sounding board to Steve and Brad or anyone else who needs me. I won't give advice, and I won't second-guess. I will be able to devote more time to meeting the needs of others, and I am looking forward to this. I think the greatest skill I have and perhaps the only skill I have that really matters is in caring for people, and I intend to continue to find ways to do this. I hope you will call on me.

The title of chairman of the executive committee means nothing; it has no authority. Although I still keenly feel the responsibility, it may take an extended period of decompression before I stop feeling responsible. It may take the rest of my life. This will be a source of some frustration to me because it is absolutely essential that Steve and Brad feel total responsibility. If they assume that I am looking over their shoulders, things will fall through the cracks. They are the ones who will have to stay awake nights now wondering if all the bases are covered.

I won't miss that part of the job, nor will I miss the title. Titles have always been more of a burden to me than a blessing, and they really don't help very much in getting things done. The only test of your leadership ability is to look over your shoulder and see if anyone is following.

The only time I would step in and interfere would be if I saw anyone violating the principles or priorities that have governed this company for over 100 years, and I don't expect this to happen. I believe that these principles are in the genes of all our family members. Steve Butler observed several years ago, "Sometimes it seems we have grown and prospered in spite of ourselves." This is an accurate statement. In spite of our recent operating setbacks, our shareholder value is at an all-time high. If we continue to operate with the same priorities and principles, if we put God, family, people, and community ahead of short-term gain, we will continue to prosper.

It's been fun, and I am looking forward to my new role because it will be fun, too. Already I'm finding the time to do some of the really important things I had been neglecting due to the press of business matters. Thank you for your support, and thank you for the support I know you will give Steve and Brad.

W. B. Turner

Bill Turner served as the third chairman of the company founded by his grandfather, W. C. Bradley. The historic cotton warehouse, listed on the National Register of Historic Places, houses the corporate headquarters of this international company. (Photo courtesy *Columbus Ledger-Enquirer*)

Giving up the leadership of the W. C. Bradley Company was harder for me than I thought it would be. Because of my big ego, I found myself being hurt because I no longer knew everything that was going on. And when I saw Brad or Steve doing something I disagreed with, I wanted to step in and meddle. Once, when I complained to Sue Marie about this, she said, "Sugar, it's just like learning to ride a bicycle. You have to let them fall off a few times to learn." My response was, "Yeah, but it's my bicycle they are tearing up."

I had to totally let go, and now Brad's and Steve's "batting average" is far better than mine. Someone asked me what new construction the W. C. Bradley Company had underway, and I said, "I don't know; because if I did, I would be telling them how to do it."

One of the things I did in order to get myself out of the way, and to please my ego, was to finally accept the invitation to join the Board of Regents of the University System of Georgia. I served for more than nine years and was fortunate to be a regent under Chancellor Stephen Portch and Governor Zell Miller. Governor Miller's strong commitment to education, coupled with Steve Portch's creative leadership, is creating in Georgia one of the finest university systems in the world. I stepped down from the Board of Regents because I felt the University System was in goods hands and because there were things I could do on the outside to make our educational system better, especially in our region. I was also feeling the nudge toward servant leadership.

I feel good about my role in life now, and it feels good to see others doing such a great job in building on the foundation that was laid for them.

Thoughts While Passing Through

- Leadership is an opportunity for service, not an opportunity for power.
- As long as we think that bad people go to hell and good people go to heaven, we're in big trouble. Heaven is for people who know they're bad but who accept God's grace.
- When people believe they are humble, they've lost it.
- Some people would rather be admired for what they appear to be than loved for who they are. The sad part is that they don't know the difference. As Alcoholics Anonymous says, "You're only as sick as your secrets." Or as Jesus says, "You're like whitewashed tombs . . . outwardly beautiful but dead on the inside."
- A person shouldn't ever retire until he has something better to do.
- When your objective becomes the perpetuation of an institution, you've lost the objective.
- There is a vast difference between success and significance.
- People may not live up to your expectations, but most will live down to your expectations.
- Our task is to tear down walls that people build to protect and replace those walls with bridges that connect.

CHAPTER 6

FILLING THE EMPTY PLACES OF MY SOUL

For I know the plans I have for you, plans for welfare and not for evil, to give you a future and a hope. Then you will call on me and come and pray to me and I will hear you. You will seek me and find me, when you seek me with all your heart.

—Jeremiah 29:11-13

By 1955 I had accomplished most of the goals in life I had set for myself. I had a lovely wife and family, a beautiful home, our business was doing well, and I was beginning to gain the respect of the community. I had held most of the civic positions that are expected of young leaders. By all standards of appearance, some of which were phony, we were a model family. But because my worth was based on performance, because of my fear of failure, because of my need to always be right, I made life miserable for those around me.

All my life I have tried to play with a stacked deck of cards to prevent failure. When I did fail, I had to place the blame on someone else because to admit failure would destroy what little self-worth I had. I have discovered, though, that failure is one of the greatest learning experiences a person can have. In fact, I can't think of one single thing I have ever learned from succeeding, but I have learned many, many lessons from falling flat on my face. Once a person accepts the fact that the world does not come to an end when he fails and that people will not desert him, he can reach out for things beyond his grasp and realize his full human potential. That's real freedom; any other freedom is only the freedom to choose your own form of slavery.

My self-examination told me that something was missing in my life, and I thought I knew what it was. I wanted the recognition that came from winning the Junior Chamber of Commerce Distinguished Service Award. Many of those whom I admired had achieved this honor. For me, it was the symbol that I had arrived. And I was certain that when I won this award, my life would be complete.

I won the award that year, but it didn't have the effect I expected. I saw how empty my life was and that status, possessions, and power wouldn't bring fulfillment. I asked myself, "What are you going to be? Are you going to spend the rest of your life seeking recognition and success? You've reached all the goals that you said you wanted. What are you going to do now?" Everybody has a need for meaning in their lives, and I saw that mine had none. In desperation I prayed for help. I can always remember the date of my life-changing experience because of the plaque I won.

Help arrived from an unlikely source. One of Sue Marie's former boyfriends invited me to a workshop at the Layman's Leadership Institute in Miami, and for some reason I went. At that meeting were successful Christian business leaders who each told a story similar to mine—only each of them had found love, joy, and peace by allowing Christ to control their lives. The night the meeting ended I prayed an honest prayer: "Lord, I really don't want to give up control of my life, but I want to want to. So, help me." That prayer started me on my journey.

What comes next needs a little explaining. I include these things to show not how great and good I am, but what God can do when we give Him permission to come into our lives. John explains all of this in his first letter:

> God is light and no shadow of darkness can exist in Him. If we say
> we have fellowship with Him and still went on living in darkness, we
> should be both living and telling a lie. But if we really are living in
> the same light in which He eternally exists, then we have true fel-
> lowship with each other and the blood of His son keeps us clean from

all sin. If we refuse to admit we are sinners, then we live in a world of illusion and truth becomes a stranger to us. But if we freely admit that we have sinned we find God utterly reliable and straight forward. He forgives our sins and makes us thoroughly clean from all that is evil. If we take up the attitude that we have not sinned, we flatly deny God's diagnosis of our condition and cut ourselves off from what He has to say to us. (1 John 1:6-10)

These verses can be illustrated by a diagram. We can choose to say that we live in Zone 1, which translates to "I may not be perfect, but compared to others my sins are not really sins." Or we can choose Zone 3, which translates to "I want what I want when I want it. No one including God is going to control my life." Or we can choose Zone 2 and allow God to live within us and His love in us to grow toward perfection (1 John 4:12).

Zone 1	Zone 2	Zone 3
No sin	The light	Habitual sin

The secret is taking the first step with commitment. It's tremendously important that we follow Jesus' example and make our commitment public so that there can be no looking back, so that all bridges are burned. What follows was my first effort to do this.

When I returned home from the layman's retreat, a minister asked me to talk about the meeting at a gathering of men of all the downtown churches. I knew that if I said "yes," there would be no going back to what I had been before. Making a public profession of faith was making a statement that I wasn't what I used to be, and I thought at the time that people would look at me a little differently. I thought I'd have to give up a lot of stuff. But you don't give up; you just keep getting.

I could have said no to the request and explained, "Oh, I don't like to talk in front of people." And I didn't. It really put a knot in my stomach to have to get up and talk. It was a real effort for me. I didn't make speeches. But the more you do it, the more comfortable you get with it—just like with anything else. It's sort of a stretching process you go through.

I was asked to repeat my talk several times, and I include it here because it was such an important step in my journey. I realize that, like most new converts, my comments sound preachy and for that I apologize, but that's the way I was at the time.

A Layman's Conceptions and Misconceptions of Christianity
Layman's Day at St. Luke Methodist Church
March 27, 1960

I was out at the St. Mary's Hills Men's Club on their program Wednesday night, and there was a newspaperman who sat next to me at supper and told me that he planned to write up the program for the paper. I asked him please not to quote anything I said because I was going to repeat myself this morning. He thought a minute and said, "Would it be all right if I just said, 'Bill Turner made some remarks and told some stories that can't be printed?' "

I hope that I won't have to place any such restrictions on what I say today. Most of you who know me know that it is a painful experience for me to get up and speak in public, and I certainly have no illusions about my ability. I had a college professor who once told me that I should do less public speaking and more private thinking, but if I can get my point over to just one person here today, it would certainly be worth the effort on my part. I received a wonderful letter from Dr. (Frederick) Porter after the Methodist Men's Club meeting in which he said that anyone could tell the number of seeds in an apple, but no one knows the number of apples in a seed. It is my hope that I can plant at least one seed.

What I really want to tell you about is an unusual meeting I attended last January. It was a meeting that I wish every layman in Columbus could have attended because, to me, it is one of the most encouraging developments to take place in this country in quite a while. But before I get into this, I would like to go back and tell you a little bit about my own conceptions of Christianity before I attended this meeting. I am doing this because I think that my conceptions are pretty well the conceptions of the average layman.

I thought about the church as being a place of worship, and you went either because you felt you wanted to go or you expected to be entertained. I also looked upon it as some sort of club where you could have fellowship with people you liked and who thought as you did. As far as the minister was concerned, I think I was inclined to place him on a pedestal and considered his calling the highest calling of God. His duties were to preach, to perform the official functions such as baptize children, to take part in marriage ceremonies, to counsel and to comfort people in trouble. But above all, his job was to win people to Christ.

As far as the layman was concerned, his duties were to support the church, to raise money when it was needed, to personally tithe, and to do whatever church work he was called upon to do. Sometimes a layman would get some special call from God to do some special task, but in the meantime he was to live by a certain code of behavior, and as long as he was moral, spiritual, temperate, and went about doing good, he was leading a Christian life.

I think sometimes we become so frantic in these efforts to go about doing good that we become completely ineffective both for ourselves and for our God. We are a lot like the story about the man who was riding down the highway on top of a great big trailer truck. He had a baseball bat in his hand, and every few minutes he would hit the top of the truck with the baseball bat, then he would run to the back end of the truck and hit it, run to the front and hit it again. Finally somebody stopped him and asked him why he was doing that. He said, "Well, this is a 10-ton truck, and I have 15 tons of chickens in here, and I have got to keep 5 of them flying all the time."

The meeting that I referred to before is called the Layman's Leadership Institute. It was a four-day gathering of Protestant laymen to study and exchange Christian ideas, experiences, and convictions. It is now in its fifth year, and each year the attendance has increased. This year 300 people were invited, and 450 attended. It was held in the Americana Hotel at Miami Beach, Florida.

I must confess that before I went down there, I thought that was a ridiculous place to hold a Christian meeting, but it was done for the express purpose of spotlighting Christianity against the background of the materialism it must defeat if Christianity is to survive in the world today. If there has ever been a monument to materialism, it is Miami Beach with all its long automobiles, furs, jewelry, and ornate buildings. Miami Beach is like the old man who made a lot of money late in life and then devoted the rest of his life trying to convince people just how rich he was. When he died, he left instructions that he was to be buried in a solid gold Cadillac. They carried out the terms of his will, and as they lowered him into the grave in that great big, long, gold Cadillac with him propped up in the back seat, a grave digger who was standing over to one side watching it said, "Umm, man. That is really living."

Our program began each morning at 8:30 with a Bible study and then lasted on through the day until 10:30 at night with a short break in the afternoon. We heard inspiring messages from many ministers such as Duke McCall, Louis Evans (who *Life* magazine says is one of the 12 outstanding religious leaders in this country), Richard Halverson, and Billy Graham.

We also heard statesmen talk about the problems Christianity faces in the world today. Governor LeRoy Collins talked about the need for Christian men in government. Senator Stuart Symington told of his recent trip to Africa and Asia and of the tremendous strategic importance of Africa in the world and of the tremendous opportunity that Christianity has because of the fact that, without exception, all of Africa's leadership today got their start in Christian mission schools. He told also of the problems we face, the fact that Islam is winning 10-1 over Christians today and how communists have 14,000 Russian-trained agents who work in Africa now and, if it follows the pattern they set in China, there will be 250,000 in a very short time.

We heard a young Russian boy named Nicholas Goncharoff talk about Christianity in Russia. He told how his father was killed and how his mother starved to death along with 97,000 other Christian leaders because they would not give up Christianity. He told of how he had to walk 300 miles to attend church, only to find a band playing outside the church so loudly that they couldn't hear what went on inside. He wound up his talk by asking the question, "Could you be a Christian in that atmosphere?"

We also attended seminars that were small enough to get to know the men and to have group discussions. We talked about Christianity from the layman's viewpoint and how to do Christian counseling and how Christianity relates to business ethics and other subjects. But to me, the thing that had the greatest impact was the laymen themselves who stood up and unashamedly told of their own Christian experiences.

There were men like Howard Butts who owns and operates 80 supermarkets in 31 different cities and yet devotes one-third of his time to lay preaching. There were men like Herbert Taylor, who is president of Club Aluminum Company and also past president of Rotary International, who told how he memorized 14 verses of scripture a day in order to have an answer to all of his problems at his fingertips. We heard a racketeer tell how he always used to look for Christians in gambling joints to justify his own actions and how he went to church the first time someone had the nerve to ask him. He pointed out the tremendous opportunity we all have that we overlook to help people find Christ. There were many others—Bill Jones (a leading industrialist), Maxey Jarman (president of General Shoe Corporation), doctors, lawyers, farmers, big men, and little men—and they had all surrendered their lives to Christ. They did not have a pious or holier-than-thou attitude but they did have a special quality about them and a warmth and vitality that was wonderful to behold, and they had all learned not to lift up their labors for men to admire but to lift up their Lord for men to love.

Now the message they told was certainly nothing new. I think you have probably all heard it from a hundred pulpits and heard it said a whole lot more eloquently. But the point I want to make is that it took a layman to change my own conception of Christianity and to make me see that while we are waiting around for special tasks from God, we all have a general duty to perform: to surrender our lives to Christ and to win others for him. These are the very basic ingredients of Christianity. We can no more have Christianity without them than we could have apple pie without apples, and with this realization the whole concept of Christianity changes.

The layman becomes the most important part of Christianity and—in addition to his other jobs I outlined—he has the major responsibility of setting an example for others, for telling other people about Christ, and for winning people to Christ. The minister still has the same duties, but outside of his official duties he does these things, not because he is a minister, but because he is a Christian just as you and I. His calling is no higher than ours, and in most cases our opportunity is far greater than his because we are in daily contact with people whom he never sees.

I went to a rather risqué play not long ago that I think illustrates both the attitude that most people have toward their minister and also the attitude they have toward themselves as laymen. As I was coming out of this play, there was one of the leading Christian laymen of Columbus in front of me. He was talking about his own minister being at the play, and he said, "I just don't think that he ought to be here. It just doesn't look right." Well, if it isn't right for the minister, then it is not right for the layman. The minister does take on one additional responsibility under this changing concept: he becomes a supply officer who furnishes us with the spiritual ammunition we need out on the battle line of life as we try as Christian laymen to win others to Christ. Christianity was a layman's movement from its beginning, and it still must be. Can you imagine where Christianity would be today if the first-century Christians had the same attitude that most of us do?

The church also changes under this new concept. In addition to being a place of worship and a place for fellowship, it also becomes a place to get your spiritual battery recharged. In short, it becomes the body of Christ, and we become its hands, its eyes, its legs, and its voice.

To me, the greatest danger the world faces today is not communism. It is not the hydrogen bomb. It is not materialism. It is Christianity practiced in the lukewarm manner that most of us practice it today with these basic ingredients missing. Now ethics are fine, and moral standards are great, but both of them are subject to erosion by comparison with the standards of others and by the pressures we live under. I think the greatest danger is to our own children, what we are doing to them with the code of ethics by which we are living. I think if you will be honest with yourself, you will admit that most children, unless the parents' code is so bad that even a child can see it and rise above it, will adopt the code of their parents, even if it is only halfway good.

I would like for each of you who have children at home to conduct an experiment. Ask your child just one question: "What is the thing our family talks about the most? What is the thing we consider of prime importance in our lives?" Now if you will do this without leading them into the answer you want them to give, I think you might be shocked and amazed at the answers they give you. I tried this in my Sunday School class not too long ago and here are some of the answers I got: bills, money, parties, politics, things. I think we are raising our children today where most of them are more concerned about getting to the moon than they are about getting to heaven. We are giving them everything in life but the thing they need most, and that is a purpose for living.

I hope you will forgive me if I give a little personal reference. I don't want anyone to get the idea that I am holding my family up as an example because we certainly have just as far to go as anybody. But this illustration will show just how a little change in the parents' attitude can make such a tremendous difference in the home.

I came back from Miami Beach determined that we were going to have a family worship service every morning. We have tried this in the past, but we have always done it hurriedly and sporadically. We would do it one morning and the next, and then maybe we would forget it for a week. Then somebody would think about it, and we would start again. But it didn't mean much to our children, and it never did mean much to us either. We talked this over with our children, and they decided they would get up half an hour earlier every morning in order that we might have time without rushing to have a family worship service.

Now three things have happened. None are very important, but at least it shows that some of this is getting through to our children. The first thing that happened was, while we were away from home recently on a trip, we came back to find that our 10-year-old daughter, Donna, had been holding family worship service every morning. When we asked her why, she said, "Well, we all wanted to; it just didn't seem right starting the day without it." The next thing that happened was my little three-year-old boy, Abbott, was over at his grandmother's trying to get her to give him a cookie before lunch. When she wouldn't do it, he told her, "Well, you just plain don't have the Holy Spirit." The third thing that happened was right before this talk was made for the first time at the Men's Club. My eight-year-old son, Brad, knew of the anxiety I was going through. As I left home, he very casually and very naturally said, "Dad, what time will you be speaking at the Men's Club?" I said, "I don't know. I guess it will be around 8 o'clock." He said, "Well, I'll be praying for you at that time." That is tremendously important to me, and it would be of tremendous importance to your own family.

You see a lot written today and everybody talks about what is wrong with marriage and why so many are failing. Thousands and thousands of words have been written about it. I think the reason for failure in marriage is very, very simple. It is the kind of people who are getting married. I would like to hold up three different types for you. There are others, but these are three that I want you to examine. One is the type that I call the "conquerors," where one mate or the other—or maybe even both—tries to impose their strong self-will upon the other mate and conquer them and grind them under and make them bend to their will. Another type is the worshiper, where either one mate or the other—or maybe both of them—worship each other until they discover that their mate has feet of clay, and the marriage fails. There is a third type I would like for you to look at, and it's the most indestructible type of all. It is a marriage where both mates have been conquered by God. It is impossible to have any selfishness in a marriage of this kind because there is no self in it. There is only a oneness, and love takes on an entirely new meaning.

In Edward Gibbon's great book, *The History of the Decline and Fall of the Roman Empire*, he lists the five major reasons why the Roman Empire fell. I would like to share them with you. Listen and see how closely they apply to America today.

- divorce and the undermining of the sanctity of the home
- rising taxes and extravagant spending
- craze for pleasure and the brutalization of sport
- the building of gigantic armaments and the failure to realize that the real enemy was already in the gates of the Empire in the moral decay of the people
- the fading of faith into a mere form, leaving people without a guide

There was an article recently in *U.S. News and World Report* that talks about what is wrong with America today. It is about 15 pages long, but I would urge every American to read that article. To sum up what they said, there are three things wrong with America. The first is that Americans won't fight for principles anymore unless they are directly affected by them. The second is that we have too much, and there is no need to strive for anything anymore. The third is a need for a goal, some challenge to shake us out of our lethargy. Now they only suggest two possible solutions. One is full-scale war, which is unthinkable, and the other is full-time Christianity, and you cannot have full-time Christianity without having full-time witnessing.

Now what does Christian witnessing really mean? You have heard this used a lot in your own churches I am sure and in various places. It means first realizing that everything we think, say, and do has an external, an internal, and an eternal effect. It means setting an example for others and it means telling people about Christ. Now I don't mean standing on the street corner on a soap box and talking, but it does mean looking for opportunities and asking God to make them known to you. If you will do this, you will be surprised at how many opportunities you pass up every day of people who want to know Christ. They are looking for something, but they don't know what it is or how to find it. It means a deliberate prayerful campaign for a specific person. Now this is too much for any of us to do. We lack the wisdom, and we lack the courage. We only create confusion both for ourselves and for the people we are trying to help. As one speaker in Miami put it, "They will become as confused as a termite in a yo-yo." But it is not too much for Christ if he walks with us, and there is only one way that he can walk with us, and that is by us surrendering our lives to him and accepting him.

The artist Holman painted a picture, *The Light of the World*. I am sure that you have all seen it. It is a picture of Christ standing outside a door and holding a lantern up over his head. When the artist had finished this picture, he showed it to one of his friends. His friend said, "That picture is not finished. The door doesn't have a handle on it." And the artist said, "Yes, it is finished. That is the door to the human heart, and it can only be opened from the inside." This is the essence of Christianity.

Why then don't we surrender our lives to Christ? There are a number of reasons. For some, it is a genuine lack of knowledge of what God wants us to do and of what God offers us in return, even though the Bible is full of the promises of joy, power, peace, abundant life, and victory over fear—even the fear of death, freedom from guilt, eternal life, and many others. These things are available for those who will accept God's gift. For others, idolatry prevents us from surrendering. Of course, idolatry is the worship of other gods, and it can take many forms. It can be money, family, power, social position, and the most vicious kind of all is the kind that is found in the church where the people worship the church or the minister as their god. Many Christians can't even get by the first commandments in being a Christian.

There is a wonderful passage of scripture in the book of Kings where the prophet Elijah really lays it on the line to his people—and he can lay it on the line to you today—in which he said, "If the Lord be God, follow him; but if Baal, then follow him." Of course, we are all familiar with the one in the New Testament where Christ says, "No man can serve two masters." Now, fear stops a lot of us, and it too can take many forms: the fear of failure, the fear of not being ready.

I never think of failure that I don't think of Babe Ruth. What is the first thing that pops in your mind when you hear the name Babe Ruth? Sixty home runs in one season? Sixty booming drives that have never been equaled and probably never will be? But most people don't realize that Babe Ruth also owns another record. Babe Ruth struck out 1,350 times.

Someone once said that a Christian is a sinner who keeps on trying. I think that one of the major stumbling blocks is the fear of being considered different, the fear of being considered a fanatic if we do what I am talking about. I think the real curse of civilization today is this Jello philosophy we all live by that says we all must conform to the same mold. If you will stop and think about it for just a second, every major advance in civilization has been made by a man who has dared to be different and who has dared to be a nonconformist. You could name a hundred: Martin Luther, John Wesley, Patrick Henry, Albert Einstein, and even the greatest nonconformist of all, Jesus Christ.

Fear of God holds a lot of us back, or rather I think it is more of a lack of trust in God. How many times have you said, after a stirring sermon and the minister asks you to come to the alter and surrender your life, "I would really like to do this, but I am afraid of what God might do with me. I've got a family. I've got a mother to support, and I've got children, and I've got a job. I am afraid that he might send me to Africa or somewhere."

I think the best way to look at that is, most of you are parents. Suppose your own child came to you and said, "Dad, I've been thinking about it. You have been very good to me, and I have really missed you lately. From now on, no matter what happens, I am going to do exactly what you say." What would you do if your child said that? Would you think, "Well now, you miserable squirt, I've got you where I want you, and from now on you are going to eat liver three times a day. You are going to spend part of each day in the closet. You are going to work in the yard until your back aches. I am going to make your life miserable from now on." Of course you wouldn't. You would probably rush out and buy everything he has been wanting the most. Of course, you would still make him go to school. You would make him take polio shots. You would make him take medicine and do other things he doesn't like, but it would be done for his own good. God loves us more than this and is infinitely wiser, and we can rest assured that His will—no matter what it might be—is the very best thing for us.

Each of our lives is like a pitcher full of water. If you wanted to pour milk into this pitcher, you must first empty it of the water. If you poured out only a small amount of the water, you would get a weak diluted mixture of milk. It is the same way with God. If you would have Him in all of His fullness and all of His richness, you must first pour out all of yourself.

How then do we reach this Christian maturity? I have always envied those who could point to the exact second when they were spiritually reborn. But for most of us, it doesn't happen this way. Even as great a Christian as John Wesley was, he was in the ministry for nearly 18 years before he surrendered his life to Christ and felt his heart "strangely warmed." For most of us, it begins with an awareness of God, an awareness of His will for us and an awareness of our shortcomings. We then ask for forgiveness, and there is a change of direction in our lives and a striving—and I underline the striving— to do His will. Christianity then becomes a growing experience and there are certain basic rules that, if you follow, will speed it along. They can best be illustrated by the word GROW.

G—Go to God daily in prayer, at the beginning, during, and at the end of each day. Start each day as an adventure by asking God the question, "What will we do today?"

R—Read the Bible daily and meditate on what you read. This is not a calisthenic but must be done prayerfully and studiously. You should have several different translations of the Bible before you and perhaps start a study course. If you do this faithfully, the Bible will take on a new meaning for you. I feel that this should be done at least one hour daily. We spend that much time on food for our body, and we need to spend a like amount of time on our spiritual food. Going to church once or twice a week no more makes us a Christian than going to a garage makes us a mechanic. We need to drill God's word into our subconscious until it becomes a part of everything we do. We need constantly to recharge our spiritual battery.

O—Obey God daily.

W—Witness for Christ by your life and your lips.

Maybe this is not all there is to it, and maybe I have over-simplified it, but I feel the same way about this that Red Skelton felt recently on a television show when he was playing the part of a cowboy. Someone asked him why he was wearing only one spur, and he answered, "I figured that if I could get one side of the horse started, the rest would come along."

I have made no attempt to prove these things. We know them in our hearts already, even if we don't admit them. The real proof is in the living, and only you can prove this for yourself. It is this simple: In each of us is a throne and a cross. If we are on the throne, then Christ is still on the cross. But if Christ is on the throne, then we must be on the cross. We spend all of our life in a mad search for the pot of gold at the foot of the rainbow and all the time it is within us at the foot of the cross.

Now I'm not one of those "Everything is wonderful since I met Jesus" kind of Christians, but I have no doubt that my life has been changed and is being changed. The writings and preaching of Father John Powell, a Jesuit priest who wrote *Why Am I Afraid To Tell You Who*

I Am?,[6] describe much of what happened to me. He talks about how the temptations of Jesus after his baptism are similar to the temptations we face in our journey through life.

Father Powell says the first temptation Satan presented to Jesus— to turn stones to bread—is the temptation to live for self-gratification, or what Sigmund Freud, the famous psychiatrist, called "the will to pleasure." I have been there and done that.

The second temptation Satan offered to Jesus was that he would make Jesus ruler of the world if he would worship him, what Adler calls the "will to power." I have learned much about power. The definition of power depends on the kind of power we're talking about. Jesus said in the first chapter of Acts that you shall receive power when you receive the Holy Spirit. That's one definition of power: the power to love and serve and glorify God. But another definition of power would be the power to lead people, control people, coerce people, manipulate people, and influence people and events.

Early in my life I probably used the second kind of power to get things done. There is a saying, "Don't ever use power unless there is no limit to the power you have." Once you start using it, you're going to have to crush somebody in order to get what you want.

I think that when you use power to get something done, somebody is going to wind up with a lasting resentment. The more you use it, the more barriers and obstacles you have out there to overcome. I think that people who get into power feel like the rules that apply to everybody else don't apply to them. Power does corrupt people. Lord Aston said, "Power tends to corrupt, but absolute power corrupts absolutely." I think that is absolutely true.

I was in a position of considerable power locally, I think. Yet I did not feel that I was effective in getting things done. I would bump up against other types of power, political or whatever. Sometimes I could influence those, and sometimes I couldn't. There was a feeling of frustration and anger. I couldn't see why people didn't agree with what I thought if my intentions were good. Why couldn't they see that I was right? And I wasn't necessarily right; I just thought I was.

There are a lot of people who say, "If I had his power or his money, I could do great things." But that's not where it comes from. It's a handicap more than anything else. I spent a lot of years with the Bradley-Turner Foundation behind me wanting to do things for Columbus, Georgia, with the attitude of "I know what's good for y'all," and I fell on my face. Good motives, but not knowing how to do it the right way.

It's a whole lot better when everyone develops a sense of ownership in what needs to get done. It takes more time, but in the long run people feel good about themselves and about what they are doing. I know that some people say I've had a major role in what has happened with the development of downtown Columbus, and yet I was never out there leading the charge. When you push power away, it just empowers everybody else, and people love that because they feel a sense of accomplishment. They connect with you, and you sort of become a funnel or a conduit for what everybody is contributing. You mix it and blend it, and it comes out to be something good, but you are not conscious of being the one who has a lot of power. When you lose your humility, you lose your power because then good and bad things can touch you.

I have seen Jesus' way work to the point where I am willing to trust him. I've never been put to the total test. But I believe enough to say I'm willing to stake my life on that. The other side—being the winner, the aggressor, looking good, being idolized, being hard—doesn't mean anything to me anymore. It used to. I don't know when that changed for me. It hasn't been all that long ago, maybe less than 20 years.

But I do know that in the 1970s something happened that proved to me I had changed. Back when Jimmy Carter was governor, he called me at home one night and asked me if I would serve on a team to deal with the race riots in Columbus. I said, "Yes, when do you want me to start?" He said, "There'll be a police car there to pick you up in 15 minutes." So, I was taken to a motel over on Rigdon Road, and there was a handful of whites and a larger number of blacks in a little motel room at tables somebody had set up. Some were good people I knew, but there were also Black Panthers who were screaming and hollering and cussing folks. One of the Black Panthers cussed me out and spit across the table at me. There was a time in my life when I would have reached over there and beat him to a pulp—and I could have done it—or I would have figured out a way to make him lose his job to pun-ish him. But I didn't feel any of that. I said, "Whoa, something has really happened to me. Something's different, and it's not fear."

Later, another of the participants sidled up to me after one of our meetings and said, "Could I come down to see you?" I said, "Yeah, come on." He said, "I'll be down there at 7 o'clock at your office. I can't come before dark." Mrs. Locke, my secretary, found out about it. I hadn't told anybody, just said I was going to be late getting home. That guy showed up, and we talked and worked out something we could do to calm it down. When he left, I looked up on the balcony above, and there were about eight Bradley Company folks standing by to protect me. Mrs. Locke was going to make sure I was all right.

Years later I was at a Pacelli High School basketball game, and as I started to leave, I heard this voice say, "Hey, Bill." It was that same man, and right in the middle of the basketball court he gave me a big bear hug. That shows you about power—the power to beat somebody up and hurt them or punish them or the power to win them through love.

According to Father Powell, the third temptation of Jesus was when Satan suggested he jump off the steeple to get people's attention. That was the temptation to deny responsibility for his own behavior, to depend totally on God to effect change. But God will never do for us what we can do for ourselves.

There was nothing basically wrong with those choices the devil offered Jesus. Jesus could have been a great world leader with power. He could have created a lot of pleasure, a lot of self-gratification if he fed everybody and made everybody happy and went around turning water into wine everywhere. Nothing was wrong with him showing that God was behind him and that he could jump off the steeple and not get hurt. Nothing wrong with those things, but it wasn't what God had in mind. Jesus rejected the temptations to choose pleasure, power, or apathy as his life principles. When we choose love as our life principle, as Jesus did, self is no longer on the throne in our life; God is on the throne. There is an emptiness in all of us that only God's love can fill. I know that after my decision to give God my life uncondition-ally, the empty spaces in my life started filling up with joy.

The only time I can remember ever letting the fear of being considered a religious fanatic stop me was in the early stages of my decision-making process when I was struggling to keep a foot in my old life, and yet knowing I would have to take the leap of faith if I ever was going to find a new life. For example, I quit drinking, but I drank Ginger ale at parties so my friends wouldn't know. Later I found out that my friends were delighted to have someone sober to drive.

I have discovered that these experiences are ways that God and I can test the depth of my commitment. This challenges us to deny self. Jesus says, "If you are ashamed of me, I will be ashamed of you." Once we make the commitment, Jesus' yoke is easy, and his light will shine through when we let him.

Everyone has the same hunger I felt. Scientist Blaise Pascal said, "There is a God-shaped vacuum in each of us that nothing else can fill." Then, when someone wants to fill the hunger and thirst in their life, all we have to do as Christians is "be ready to give a reason for the hope that is in you, but do it with gentleness and reverence" (1 Pet 3:15). We don't have to go around pretending to be Christians. We don't have to go around asking people if they are saved.

In my early Christian days, when the minister would ask people to come to the altar to give their lives to Christ, I used to peek to see if any of those were people I'd talked to, and I'd count the number that came down. I felt like they were scalps I could hang on my belt to prove God was using me. That was my preoccupation with performance again. What I believe now is that God's spirit is in us. His light will shine through, and people will see the difference. That's what happened to me. I saw people with something I didn't have, and I wanted it to fill the emptiness (Matt 14–16). Later, when people asked what had changed for me, I was able to tell them (1 Pet 3:15). When an old college friend who hadn't seen me in 20 years said to me, "Didn't you used to be Bill Turner?" I knew I was making progress.

Thoughts While Passing Through

- Meaning is a basic human hunger man cannot live without for very long. Meaning comes from loving God by loving one another.
- It is so easy to get into the habit of trying to keep our days full when the real problem is that our lives are empty.
- It even took Jesus all night to pray, "Thy will be done."
- God can't forgive what we refuse to admit. This is the core source of broken relationships because we can't forgive others if forgiveness hasn't gotten through to us.
- When I dress or act in a way to win your approval, I'm treating you as a mirror, but if I don't care what you think, I'm treating you as a broken, blank wall. When we're both broken, we can see what God sees.
- The purpose of confession is not to grovel before God and beg for forgiveness. Forgiveness is already there. The purpose is so that we might fully understand unconditional love (grace).
- The cure for pride is praising God.
- Can we love one person unconditionally unless we love all people unconditionally?
- The existence of God is not the issue. The issue is the difference He can make in our lives.
- The biggest mistake we make as disciples is trying to hand the gospel down instead of getting on our knees, washing feet, and loving and serving others. Some people mistake their zeal for the Great Commission by trying to make disciples. We don't make disciples. Our task is the great commandment to "love one another as I have loved you." The commandment was given before the commission.

CHAPTER 7

WHAT LOVE CAN DO

> *His gifts unto men are varied. Some he made his messengers, some prophets, some preachers of the gospel, to some he gave the power to guide and teach his people. His gifts were made that Christians might be properly equipped for their service, so that the whole body might be built up until the time comes when, in the unity of faith and common knowledge of the Son of God, we arrive at real maturity—the measure of development which is meant by "the fullness of Christ."*
>
> —Ephesians 4:11-13 (Phillips)

It used to trouble me that I never received a "burning bush" kind of call from God. I suppose I was most troubled by the story about the rich young ruler who was told to sell all he had and give it to the poor and then follow Jesus. My rationalization persuaded me that the rich young ruler put possessions ahead of Jesus. I don't believe this is true in my case. I have tithed for most of my life and do my giving in prayer and partnership with God. I try to be a good steward and usually give away 50% or more of my income each year. I don't say this boastfully because I don't miss a dime I have given. But sometimes I feel that I may have tried to work out compromises with God in order to stay where I am with my position and with my family, offering God "goodies" rather than myself. However, looking back, I believe that God has given me a great platform for launching things for Him.

The Bible is a history of the love that waits. It is also a history of God who empowers ordinary people to do extraordinary things when they respond to His love. I believe that when God calls us to ministry, He equips us for it. That is what faith is all about, and that is what has happened to me. I believe that God provides me with the experiences and resources that lead me to the service where He wants me.

I never realized that I was being equipped for service until I took the first step. A golfer never knows he or she has the talent to play golf until he/she tries and tries and tries. It's the burning desire to play that motivates the golfer, or perhaps the desire to emulate someone he admires. Natural ability is a gift, but ability also comes through practice and through trial and error. It's only after we begin the journey that we know that God guides and equips us every step along the path. It's only when we look back in retrospect that we begin to understand that God has given us the gifts and the experiences to bring us to where we are, and that He has rewarded us and is preparing us for the rest of the journey. What follows are some of the gifts God has given me.

The Gift of the Spirit

God certainly used an ignoble beginning to point me in the direction He wanted me to go. Upon my return from the Navy I was flying pretty high. I think my dad was concerned enough about my behavior to talk to our minister about me. My dad would seldom confront me about my negative behavior, but he would let me know in a variety of ways that he expected the best from me. This was in some ways a good practice because people usually will live down to others' expectations, but only sometimes will live up to them. The bad side is that if we don't face up to the reality of a situation, we encourage phoniness. This had certainly been true in my case.

Our minister at St. Luke invited me to lunch one day—I'm sure my dad was behind it—and asked me to teach a fifth grade Sunday School class. I told him that I was neither intellectually nor spiritually equipped to take on the task. He replied, "All I ask of you is that you be real. And when you talk about Jesus, tell only what you know and know that you know, and you'll be amazed at how your knowledge will increase."

I said I would do it, partially because I thought that being a Sunday School teacher would look good on my résumé and partially to get Dad off my back, but also because I was aware of an emptiness in my life and thought I might give it a try. Initially I followed my minister's advice, and because I knew so little about Jesus, I talked more about Lou Gehrig and Babe Ruth. But an amazing thing began to happen. I found that I could connect with the kids and that I cared deeply for them. As I've come to know, this is what happens every time we are exposed to the love of Christ.

I wanted to be a good influence on them, which initially meant being more careful and circumspect in my behavior. I was a pretty heavy smoker. It was after I started teaching Sunday School that a retired minister—Edward Grimes, I'll never forget him—came up to me at St. Luke and put his arm around me and said, "You're doing a wonderful job with these kids"—and he patted me on the shirt pocket where my cigarettes were—"but these things have to go; you're a bad influence." I threw them away that night and have never smoked another one. To help me quit, I wrote a list of the reasons I wanted to stop smoking and put it in my shirt pocket. Whenever I wanted a cigarette, I'd feel up there and pull out that note.

My co-teacher was Louise Starling, a wonderful lady, and together we found a creativity in me I never knew I had, and that creativity sparked creativity in the kids. We built a bas-relief map of Palestine and Nehemiah's wall. We produced a newspaper, The Jerusalem Times —The Good News, with stories related to Jesus' life. We even had a beehive in our classroom until an official board member was stung going to church. I have learned since then that creativity is contagious wherever it is allowed to exist.

One of my early mentors was Mills Lane, CEO of C&S Bank. Mills was one of the most innovative, creative people I have ever known, but he did some really crazy things. He would quickly admit his mistakes, laugh loudly at his foolishness, and be off in another direction with another creative idea. The C&S organization knew that failure wasn't fatal because of Mills' example, and because of this they were not afraid to be creative themselves, and together they created a new way of banking in Georgia.

To celebrate Bill Turner's 50th year of teaching Sunday School, a bronze statue of him teaching was presented to St. Luke United Methodist Church. The sculpture was cast by Carl Porter and mounted by Norris Randall. On the sculpture's ring finger is a shiny gold band that recognizes the significant role his wife, Sue Marie, played in Bill's ongoing commitment to ministering to youth.

Teaching fifth grade Sunday School made me learn to study the Bible. It was in preparation for the nudge I would receive to take on the infamous senior high class where the average tenure of a teacher was three months.

I wanted to turn down the assignment to teach the senior high class because I didn't feel I had anything to offer. I found that I needed those teenagers just as much as they needed me. They asked probing questions. They presented difficult problems. They searched for meaning. They challenged everything I said to them.

These young people continue to disturb, confuse, and perplex me, but in a good way. In their search for meaning and truth they shake every belief I have that can be shaken, but what is left is good and solid and can be built upon. I hear them say, "Listen to us. We don't ask that you agree. Just listen and rethink your own position." Secretly, I think they want me to be right.

In the 50-plus years I have taught, I have never, ever had to ask a student to be quiet or to leave the room. Such is the power of the gift God gives us when we say "yes" to Him. My agreeing to teach was not my gift to God; it was His gift to me. Teaching these young people has truly changed my life. Jesus says, "Give and it will be given unto you, full measure, pressed down, and overflowing" (Luke 6:38). These young people have propped me up and loved me through many a bad situation. They have encouraged me, accepted me, and enabled me so that God's love might overflow into other areas of my life. What I have learned through teaching has made me more able at home, at work, and in the community. These young people have given me the love that allows me to be real, not a phony person. They have taught me how to be a better parent, and they have given me the discipline to study and read the Bible. I would never have studied so hard if I weren't preparing to teach.

The teacher always learns more than the student. My ongoing experience with teenagers has been a constant learning experience. I learned that the way I related to my Sunday School class was not consistent with the way I treated my own family. It's easy to be a good person with someone you don't live with, someone who doesn't really know what you are like. It's also easier to be more transparent and vulnerable with those who cannot remind you of your own shortcomings. One of my own kids told me once, "You judge us by our actions, but judge yourself by your intentions." Wow! "Judge not that you be not judged."

I have learned that each person we meet wears an invisible sign that says, "Make me feel loved." I believe that Jesus' ability to make people feel loved is what made the disciples drop their nets and follow him. I believe, as John Steinbeck said, that all sin is an attempted shortcut to love.

If you have to ask "Why am I loved?" you don't understand the kind of love Jesus was talking about. If you feel loved because you are pretty, what about when you are not pretty? If you feel loved because you are kind, what about when you are mean? If you feel loved because you are good, what about when you are bad? If you feel loved because you are interesting, what about when you are dull? If you feel loved because you are strong, what about when you are weak? If you feel loved because you are a success, what happens when you fail? Performing to please others, to win their love, doesn't work because you feel used, not loved. There is no admission price on Jesus' kind of love.

Love is sharing your true self and modeling what you want to see happen. When I share with you not only what I want to do but also what I feel, you begin to know who I am. If I want you to really know me, I could tell you that I am a husband and a father and a businessman and a Methodist, but there are thousands of these. But when I tell you that I am driven to seek praise and approval from others in order to feel love, when I tell you that I am driven to perform in order to feel worthwhile because in early childhood I learned to equate love with performance, and when I tell you that some days I feel like the town pump because everyone makes demands upon me and then other days I feel useless because no one makes demands on me, and then some other days I feel torn in multiple directions because of the conflicting demands I cannot satisfy that people make upon me, then you begin to understand who I am, and then you will respond because the most precious gift one person can give to another is his true self. I must do this in order to know real love, or I'll think you love me for what I pretend to be rather than what I really am.

Jesus said to "love one another as I have loved you." In Paul's letter to the Ephesians he wrote:

> I pray that you, rooted and firmly fixed in love yourself, may be able to grasp with all Christians how wide and long and deep and high is the love of Christ and to know for yourself that love so far beyond and above our understanding. May you be filled through all your being with God Himself. (3:16-19)

I believe that Jesus expects us to love and serve all people who come between us and God in all areas of our lives. If we want to love God, we must literally love God though all the people between us and Him. It is not enough for me to love the lovely, my beautiful family, my beautiful Sunday School class, and my beautiful friends. Jesus doesn't leave that option open to me. He says that even the Pharisees do that. I must love the unlovely whom God puts between me and Him, even those who persecute me, and I must do it now because the only way to change behavior is to begin immediately.

Love is not a feeling; it's an act of will. The person whom God puts in front of me for me to love may not be lovely or loveable at the time, but when I begin to act loving over and over again, even when I don't feel like it, three things will happen. First, my feelings will change toward the other person. Second, the other person will change. And third, the other person will begin to understand the wonder of God's love for me, even when I don't deserve it.

The tragedy in this life is not dying. It is not even in a short life. The real tragedy is wasting even one moment without experiencing God's love flowing into us and through us toward others. The real tragedy is letting someone die without knowing God's love through us. God pours oceans of love into us and through us to enable us to reach out and love as He loves. Nothing can come close to touching this experience. Once we experience this love, we'll never go back to being what we were before.

Scott Peck, in *A Road Less Traveled*,[7] said that love is a commitment to extend oneself to nurture the spiritual growth of another. This statement is a test of any loving relationship we might have. This is Jesus' kind of love and, boy, did he extend himself for you and me!

In my Sunday School classes at Christmas time I teach a lesson about covenants: God's covenant (Yahweh—"I will be for you."); Emanuel (God in you/with you); Jesus' covenant in John 14:18 ("I will not leave you alone or desolate. I will come to you."); and my covenant ("You've got a friend"). I give each person a Bible. Inside the Bible is a slip of paper that says, "You've got a friend" and on this piece of paper is a commitment to them from Jesus and also one from me to be with them always, to be for them always. I play Carol King's song "You've Got a Friend." I love the line that goes, "Winter, spring, summer, or fall, all you got to do is call, and I'll be there." Nothing the student can say or do will ever change that. Even when I don't feel like loving them, I'm their man. If they need someone to be tender, I will be tender. If they need someone to be tough, I'll be tough. If they need someone to listen, I'll listen. When they are in the pits, I'll go to them. How do I know I'll do this? Because someone did it for me first, and I claim the promises Jesus made to be with me always and give me a never-ending supply of love.

I have learned that when anyone experiences tough, unconditional love, they will change. I've seen this happen to poor students, drug addicts, promiscuous and rebellious teenagers, and prisoners. Some years ago Carl Rogers, the famous psychologist, revolutionized counseling when he discovered that people who went to him with different symptoms—alcoholism, sexual promiscuity, depression, and other things—all had the same problem, and when they understood and accepted and loved themselves, they gave up the symptoms. No one can do this for themselves until someone else does it for them first.

When young people first began coming to me with their problems, I usually gave them a lecture. If they said they had been drinking, I would lecture them on drinking. If they said they were depressed, I would tell them that a Christian shouldn't feel that way because they had so much to be thankful for. All I was doing was affirming the low opinion they already had of themselves, and they either went back into their shell or never came back. But when I learned to separate the person from the behavior and to love the person—even when I hated the behavior—and when I learned to try to understand why this person was in pain or why they felt empty, then they too began to love and accept and understand themselves and began to change. That is the kind of love Jesus is talking about. It is the kind of love Paul talks about in Hebrews when he tells us we have a high priest who understands because he was tempted as we are tempted.

God equips us by the gift of the Holy Spirit and by leading us to the body of Christ. The Sunday School classes I've taught for more than 50 years constitute my body of Christ. When God called me to teach an unruly senior high Sunday School class, He gave me an incredible love for teenagers that I didn't know I had, and it's a love that allows me to be vulnerable to them. I believe that in my earlier life God was equipping me to use my experiences, both good and bad, to minister to these young people.

At one point I seriously considered leaving the company and becoming a counselor. Through my exposure to workshops at the Bradley Center and the Pastoral Institute, I had been exposed to some of the best people in the field. It wouldn't have taken long to get my master's degree in counseling. Then it struck me that there was a reason why I was able to help troubled kids. When they came to my office, they saw how busy I was. They saw the work piled on my desk. They heard the phone ringing, and when they left, they usually saw people waiting to see me—business executives, college presidents, ministers, government officials—and they would think: "Hey, he gave me an hour. He must care. I must be somebody." Carl Rogers once said that when people find love and acceptance, they change. That's what I had going for me. That's what I would give up had I left my position to go into counseling.

The love that Paul struggles to describe has its source in God. In fact, it is the gift of God to us. It may be found in the Christian home if you are fortunate. It is also found in the body of Christ, the church. Upon graduation my students leave this source of love and enter a world that seems to be ruled by hate and violence, a world with its values turned upside down, a world that seems preoccupied with craze for pleasure and escape from reality.

I saw some figures from "Youth for Christ" that said in an hour's time 188 teenagers will seek help for drinking problems, 14 unwed teenagers will give birth to babies, 22 teenagers will seek abortions, and 29 teenagers will attempt suicide. More than 50% of young people today will suffer from depression at one time or another. I always encourage my students with all earnestness to find or start a Christian caring community wherever they go. I think their very survival depends on this, and so does the survival of our world.

It is only in the body of Christ that we find love that fills the emptiness we are tempted to fill with booze, sex, success, popularity, and recognition. It is only in the body of Christ that we can find love to enable us to know ourselves, to accept ourselves, to be ourselves, and to forget ourselves. It is only in the body of Christ that we can find love that is not based on performance.

Becoming a part of the body of Christ is absolutely necessary, for it is only here that we will find the courage to face our doubts and the rejection and pain that come with loving as Jesus loves. This kind of love begins with forgiveness.

Love is about forgiveness. There is a true story about a bishop in the Philippines who interviewed a girl who claimed to talk to Jesus. After questioning her, the bishop said, "There is one sure way I can know if what you say is authentic. The next time you talk to Jesus, ask him what was the last thing I confessed to him and asked his forgiveness for." The girl came back in due course, and the bishop asked her "Did you talk to Jesus?" "Yes, I did." "Did you ask him what was the last thing I did that I asked him forgiveness for?" "Yes, I did." "And what did Jesus reply?" "He said, 'I've forgotten.' "

That is the kind of love that Jesus has for you and me. He buries our iniquities in the deepest part of the sea and remembers them no more. This is what he commands us to do, not to store up grievances to be pulled out and thrown at another person in rage when it will hurt the most. We are not to pull back the scab on our old wounds to see if they are healing, but we are charged to forgive and forget.

My students have taught me to listen carefully, to listen between the lines. As Carl Rogers wrote, "When a person is deeply heard, there is a moisture in his eyes. . . . Thank God someone listened. Thank God that someone knows what it's like to be me." I learned as Rogers wrote, "In my relationship with persons I have found that it does not help in the long run to act as though I were something that I am not." It blows a kid's mind to see an adult be real! We have raised a generation of zombies who have learned that many feelings are not acceptable. I have learned that feelings cannot be selective and that if we push feelings down, eventually we feel nothing at all. I have had many kids come to me and tell me their parents were getting a divorce and that this was the first indication they had that anything was wrong.

I have learned that the teenagers I work with see me differently than do most of my peers. In the time I have been teaching I have had numerous young people come to me who were suicidal. Thank God, someone got to them in time. I have broken in a house to get to a young person who called me after overdosing on pills. I have lost count of how many young people have come to me telling me of their depression and pain and that they were contemplating suicide. And yet I have lost four good friends of my own generation to suicide, one of those being my college roommate. The lesson here is obvious. One, my young people know of my weaknesses, and they know of the pain I have had in my own life, and they know I will understand their pain. And two, my young people know I love them. Those closer to my own age don't see me the same way. They see me as someone who has it all together and won't understand their pain. That made me want to be a more authentic person so people will know who I am. You don't lose anything by being real.

I heard a great Christian leader tell of how his little son burst into his study one morning while he was having his quiet time of prayer, and he angrily ran the little boy out. He heard his son ask his mother, "Why does Daddy shut himself up like this every morning?" And then he heard his wife's sarcastic reply, "So that he can love everyone downtown." I know that hits home with me. It is difficult to love in all areas of your life all the time. When we try to compartmentalize our lives and act differently in different situations, we get in trouble.

C. S. Lewis in *The Screwtape Letters*[8] nailed this kind of behavior when he had the devil, Screwtape, tell the apprentice devil, Wormwood, as they discussed strategy as to how to win a "patient to the kingdom below":

> Do what you will; there is going to be some benevolence, as well as some malice, in your patient's soul. The great thing is to direct the malice to his immediate neighbors . . . and to thrust his benevolence out to the remote circumference. The malice thus becomes wholly real and the benevolence largely imaginary.

We think we've got to keep up this façade of being perfect, but we don't. We're all in the same boat. Everybody's just alike. We've all got the same feelings and hurts, maybe a little bit different, but I can relate to yours, and you can relate to mine. That's what I try to teach in Sunday School, to get those kids to recognize that they are not weird because they feel the way they do. That's just the way we are.

And I learned another truth in this class where I'm supposed to be the teacher. Like all great truths, I wondered why I hadn't discovered it before because it is so simple and obvious. One Sunday we were talking about people and the qualities that make them trustworthy. In the discussion we discovered that the people we trusted were both open and caring. This led us to discover that trusting included the risk of being hurt, but that the hurt from trusting was not nearly as painful as the loneliness of not trusting. This led us to discover that if we wanted others to trust us, we must first be willing to trust others. (What an admission for a parent to make!) Therefore, before we can trust others, we must first trust ourselves. And before we can trust ourselves, we must trust God. And we learn to trust God through trusting others and ourselves. It's a circle held together by love, with love a part of trust and trust a part of love. Then it dawned on me: God trusts me! "And the light still shines in the darkness and the darkness has never put it out." Never!

Like most people, I much prefer not to think of my death. But as I get older, I find the fear is not as great. I think that's part of the way God intended it. I feel that the way we treat people, we make our own heaven and hell. Jesus wrote about the kingdom of heaven being now, in our midst. But he also said it's coming. I think we are in a process. I think all the way to heaven is heaven, and all the way to hell is hell, and we're headed in one direction or the other. We are on a road toward preparation to perfection. We won't see perfection until we see the face of Jesus. I'm a long way from perfection. The beauty is that God provided for it with the forgiveness that comes through Jesus. We can mess up today, but that doesn't mean we can't get a fresh start tomorrow. I emphasize this in my Sunday School class. My students say, "You've been a Christian this long, and you're still struggling this hard?" I say, "Yeah, I am, but I'm not going back to what I was. I'm going to keep on trying."

In all situations we must learn to know ourselves, accept ourselves, share ourselves, and forget ourselves. We must feel a mission to build self-worth in others. Our values must be the same in all situations, and we must have a passion for souls. God has given me the people I need to teach me the lessons I must learn—a wife who won't let me be anything but real, who is real herself, who models compassionate caring for family and others. And God has given me a place to practice what I learn—at home, at Sunday School, in business, and in the community.

My students have taught me the meaning of unconditional love. Their love and support helped me to become a real person and to face and accept my humanness and imperfections. They taught me that I am needy and must receive as well as give love. They've taught me why I must belong to the body of Christ and have a place to come when I hurt, when I doubt, or when my cup needs filling. They have shown me what the body of Christ can be and have become the body of Christ for me. They have helped me to find God, for God is love. And they have given me faith, hope, and love.

I've also learned that I have to practice what I preach. A number of years ago Sue Marie and I took the Brookstone School tennis team to Chattanooga, Tennessee, to play, and after supper we were walking back to our motel. As we passed a tavern, we heard a woman scream and then saw a man dragging her by her legs out of the tavern to a car. A large, young man wearing a University of Tennessee jacket was coming in the opposite direction, and I said to him, "Let's break that up." His reply was, "Not me." I walked up to the man with the woman and said, "Let her go." He said, "Butt out, Buddy." I said, "Look, let's be reasonable. You're going to have to turn her loose when we fight. I don't grow skin nearly as fast as I used to, and I don't want to fight, but I promise you if you don't let her go, you'll have knots all over your head. So why don't you save both of us a lot of pain?"

He looked at me for what seemed like 20 minutes, and when he saw I meant it, he threw the woman aside, saying "She's not worth fighting for,"and jumped into his car and scratched off. The woman scrambled back into the tavern crying.

Later in the motel room when I realized what I had done, I began to shake all over. I asked myself, "Why did you do such a foolish thing when he could have pulled a knife or a gun and killed you?" I don't believe I did it because of the woman. I believe I did it because I didn't want the students in my Sunday School class to see me not living up to what I had been teaching. My only regret is that I didn't follow the woman into the tavern and tell her, "You are worth fighting for because Jesus said so."

I have learned other things while teaching young people. For example,

- Young people respond better to an action than they do to a speech.

- Young people respond to realness and reject phoniness. They appreciate openness and will not betray a trust.

- Young people are looking for identity, meaning, and purpose and want to believe there is hope for the future.

- Young people are looking for caring people who will accept them as they are, and when they find acceptance, they are willing to change. Their acceptance has enabled me to change and grow.

- Young people, like other humans, have a great need to express their feelings, but need to learn how to do this constructively without hurting themselves or others. Adults can do much to help them with encouragement, patience, and example.

- Young people have a great need to belong and cannot resist genuine love. Genuine love can overcome any mistake an adult makes as a parent, teacher, or friend.

- Young people will listen and evaluate my beliefs if I will really listen to theirs. They have taught me to listen more objectively to my own children and to hear better what they are saying. I wish every parent could have the experience of learning with teenagers.

- Young people are not a finished product, but they are in the process of "becoming." They have helped to keep my own beliefs from becoming set in concrete. They have given me the freedom to fail and the ability to learn from the experience.

- Young people have taught me that I can't outgive God, for whatever I have given to young people has been returned to me a hundred times over. I wish I had more to give, for I know of no other investment that promises a greater return.

- Young people have given me hope for the future and a reason for being. They have taught me that the kingdom of heaven is now and that I really must come as a child to enter it—and enjoy it forever.

My hope is that my students realize how good they are and how good they can become and what the world would be like if they acted on their goodness. If each person only loved one person into a loving relationship with Christ in six months and that process was repeated by each of the new recruits, in 18 years the whole world would be Christian. It takes courage to listen to your goodness and to act on it, but that's what faith is—accepting love to be able to love. Jesus tells us, "Love one another as I have loved you. I have told you these things so that my joy may be in you and your joy may be complete."

I've had my moments of doubt. The director of Christian education at St. Luke asked me to "teach the teachers" what I do in my class. My first reaction was, "If I give away all my lessons and ways to get the students involved, they will attract the kids that I had been attracting." My second reaction was to wonder what I would use if others were using my lesson plans. Then it occurred to me that unless I am willing to give all that I have and unless I fully believe that my resources will be replenished by the Holy Spirit, I have no business teaching.

There have also been many times when I've questioned whether I was making an impact on these kids, and I would ask God to show me what He wanted me to do. The answer I've kept getting is that I'm right where He wants me to be. Sometimes God wants us to bloom where we're planted. I believe Romans 8:28-30:

> And we know that in all things God works for the good of those who love him, who have been called according to His purpose. For those God foreknew he also predestined to be conformed to the likeness of his Son, that he might be the firstborn among many brothers. And those he predestined, he also called; those he called, he also justified; those he justified, he also glorified.

The Gift of Community

I have found that there is more to being a Christian than just accepting Christ into my life. There is a great need to be part of a fellowship of forgiven sinners, what Paul calls the "body of Christ." In Ephesians 4:1-16 Paul describes this need. For me in my early days, this body was a prayer group made up of other "baby Christians" who began meeting on Mondays for lunch after the Lay Witness Mission at St. Luke.

Included in our group were Tap Hanson, the leader of the Lay Witness Weekends and director of the W. C. Bradley Company Human Resource Department, Mote Andrews, Tom and Billy Cunningham, Buddy Flournoy, Jim Hendrix, Walter Braun, and me. Later, Bill Henson, pastor of Wynnton Methodist Church, and Jim Jackson, pastor of St. Mark Methodist Church, joined our group. I've always believed that these two ministers came partly because of their need to be in a small group fellowship and partly because of their need to see Christian laymen taking their faith seriously. Paul explains that a small group fellowship is needed because each person is given different gifts by the Spirit, and each gift is needed if we are to grow into the "fullness of Christ." We also need to hear the "truth spoken in love." After our group broke up, my Sunday School class began to fill this need for me.

I try to illustrate the importance of small group fellowship to my Sunday School students with a lesson I teach at the beginning of class each year. I give each person a paper cup and ask them to pour out the things in their lives that keep them from being filled with the undiluted love of Jesus. I explain that the thing I need to pour out is pride and the reluctance to ask for help in getting my needs met. Then I ask each person to punch holes in their cup to symbolize the things that keep them from being filled with "living water" (John 4:10; 7:37-38). My own example is the fear of rejection and fear of failure. Then I pour water into each person's cup, and of course, it quickly runs out. Then I stack the cups together and pour water in, and none leaks out. When we are one in the Spirit, our weaknesses are overcome, and we can give a drink to a thirsty world.

The Gift of Compassion

Another way that God equips us is by teaching us to use all of our life experiences in ministry to others, especially the experiences we have had with pain. This is the meaning of Romans 5:3-4,

> More than that, we rejoice in our suffering, knowing that suffering produces endurance, and endurance produces character, and character produces hope and hope does not disappoint us because God's love has been poured into our hearts through the Holy Spirit that has been given to us.

I have not fully reached this point yet, but I agree with William Barclay: "Endurance is not just the ability to bear a hard thing, but to turn it into glory." I believe that we can use our pain and suffering to minister to others with a love that glorifies God.

All of us can expect pain in our lives. The Sermon on the Mount tells us that "he who hears these words of mine and does them is like a wise man who builds his house upon a rock and the rains came and the winds blew and beat upon the house." Jesus didn't say *if* the rains come; he said "the rains came." Life is tough. Bad things happen. The question is not "Why do bad things happen?" but "What do we do when bad things happen?" There are only three things we can do. We can nurse our pain, we can rehearse our pain, or we can immerse our pain in service to others. I think using our pain to help others is the way to go. What better person to minister to a bereaved person than one who has known grief? It takes courage to grieve properly. What better person to minister to someone who is ill than someone who has known illness? What better person to minister to someone with an infirmity than someone who has experienced an infirmity? It takes courage to use our weakness to enable God to show His strength. Former Georgia Secretary of State and U.S. Senator Max Cleland, a handicapped veteran, is a perfect example of someone whom God has made stronger at the broken places. The key to the success of Alcoholics Anonymous is one wounded person helping another wounded person to heal.

Several years ago I had a young girl in my Sunday School class who had a terrible tragedy in her life. I can't describe the tragedy without identifying the girl, but she spent many Sundays after our Sunday School class pouring out to me her guilt, her sense of loss, her anger, and her sadness. But then she heard of a young man whom she scarcely knew who had experienced a similar tragedy, and she wrote him a letter and told him she knew what he was going through and that if he would like to talk, she would come by. She went to him. As she reported to me later, "All we did was stand there and cry, and then we held each other and cried some more. And then what seemed like 30 minutes later, we began to talk. But somehow the healing began for both of us."

Tex Rhoden is another example of this. When I came back from the Layman's Leadership Institute, I began attending a new Bible study at St. Luke with several other new Christians. We were soon joined by several ministers who, I believe, came because they needed a place where they could be real people and get off the pedestal where most people put them. I believe that they also came because they needed the encouragement of ordinary laypeople who were trying to take their religion seriously.

Our fame—or was it our peculiarity—spread, and we were asked to speak at the chapel program at Goodwill Industries. I don't remember anything I said because of a sour-faced, cynical little man sitting in a wheelchair in the back of the room. That man was Tex Rhoden, and one of our group members invited and later brought Tex to our Monday Bible study. Tex let us know right away that he was there for the free lunch, which consisted of two slices of bread, mayonnaise, a slice of cheese, potato chips, and a Coke. Tex had the kind of personality that could light up a room just by his leaving it, and he was an agnostic at best, and probably an atheist. But he had a quick mind, and his questions of us were incisively probing and cynical. I realize now that he was testing us.

One day at the close of our meeting Tex said, "If you are what you say you are, you would raise the money for my operation so that I could walk." We raised the money, but we also went the second mile. We knew that because of his cerebral palsy Tex would have a rough time, and we committed ourselves to round-the-clock nursing. For the first few days Tex was in and out of consciousness. I can remember leaving the hospital at 4 AM after a four-hour shift where I fed and washed and cleaned up after Tex, feeling that was the closest I had ever come to being the servant God wanted me to be.

Tex still needed crutches to walk, and he remained the same feisty, cynical person in many ways. He said, "If you still believe in this prayer stuff, pray that I can get a car, learn to drive, get a job, and be self-sufficient. We got him an old Volkswagon, put what we used to called a "necking knob" on the steering wheel so his crippled hand would fit, taught him to drive, and presented him to the license examiner for a driving license. Because Tex had a way of looking sideways to see straight ahead, his driving test was probably the quickest on record. The W. C. Bradley Company gave him a job in our data processing department, and I have always been proud of the way our people made sure that Tex would succeed. Tex sold a house in Texas that he had inherited from his mother and bought a mobile home that one of our group members, Bob Culpepper, customized for a handicapped person.

One day Tex came to our Monday meeting and said, "There is one other thing I want you to do for me. I want all of you to stand with me next Sunday at St. Luke when I am baptized into the Christian faith." I can still see him kneeling at the altar in bright red socks.

Tex shared with me that the reason for his cynicism was that he had watched his mother burn to death in a grease fire over her kitchen stove and that he had been unable to get up and help her. Tex went on to get a degree in counseling from Auburn University and became a rehabilitation counselor at Goodwill Industries. He later worked for the State of Alabama.

He sent me a long, handwritten letter that I still have and treasure. It must have taken him hours to write it. In the letter he said,

> First of all, I am much happier than I have ever been in my life. I think you know, Bill, that one of my main desires in life was to be able to feel like I was contributing to my world instead of just taking from it. I feel that way now, and a large part of that feeling has come from my work with the Bradley Company. . . . It seems to me, Bill, that we are all programmed from childhood to be the leader, the man up front, the chief, rather than just another Indian. . . . Bill, the improvement in my sense of self-worth and peace of mind has been at least 100%. This feeling, plus the counseling I received at Athens, has convinced me that I have finally found what I have been looking for—a place to make my unique contribution. I believe my history of achievement proves that I have as much ambition as any man, but I am ambitious to be what God designed me to be, not someone else's perception, not even my own, and by His grace I fully intend to make it. That's what I got from the sharing group at St. Luke, and it literally saved my life. My life has been changed. You prayed that I would be healed, but I have been healed far greater than you will ever know. I have been healed on the inside. I am no longer an emotional cripple. I have become what God wanted me to be.

Tex lost his life in an automobile accident shortly after his letter. As he lay in a coma before he died, people came from all over Alabama and Georgia to tell us how Tex had used his pain to serve them and change their lives. His loving spirit had set their hearts aflame!

I have had many experiences in my life, but there is no experience that can compare with the joy of letting God use me to be part of the transforming of another person. I still have a picture of Tex where I see it every morning to remind me of this.

Can we expect anyone to experience God's love through us if we fail to show our wounds? If Christ hadn't been wounded, would we feel forgiven and loved? There is a true story of a young Catholic priest named Father Damien who went to a leper colony in Hawaii where he preached and nursed the lepers in the hospital. But it wasn't until he stood in the pulpit and showed the tell-tale spots of leprosy on his hands and began his sermon by saying, "My fellow lepers," that the lepers came to know Christ in their own lives.

There is a poem that haunts me, and I hope it haunts you, too. It's by Amy Carmichael, an Irish woman who became a missionary in the mid-1800s and spent 53 years in Southern India rescuing children who had been dedicated by their families to be temple prostitutes. It goes like this:

> Hast thou no scar?
> No hidden scar in foot, or side, or hand?
> I hear thee sung as mighty in the land,
> I hear them hail thy bright ascending star,
> Hast thou no scar?

> Hast thou no wound?
> Yet I was wounded by the archer spent,
> Leaned Me against a tree to die; and rent
> By ravening beasts that encompassed me, I swooned:
> Hast thou no wound?

> No wound? No scar?
> Yet, as the Master shall the servant be,
> And pierced are the feet that follow Me;
> But thine are whole: can he have followed far
> Who has not wound nor scar?[9]

We come to this place as little children, limping from broken dreams. We come nursing old wounds that will not heal. We come with the faint hope that somehow Jesus will bear our grief and sorrow and heal our wounds. And we hear Jesus say, "Love one another as I have loved you. I have told you these things that My joy might be in you and your joy might be complete."

Although our family has been tremendously blessed, we have suffered some significant losses. The deaths of my parents and Sue Marie's shook us to the core, as did the deaths of Mark Moshell, the husband of our daughter Marie, and Bradley Brown, the infant son of our daughter Donna and her husband, David Brown.

We all face tragedy in our lives. Remember, Jesus didn't say *if* the rains fell and the clouds came and the wind blew. He said *when* this happens. Part of my decision to commit my life to Christ was based on the certain knowledge that with a family as large as mine, the law of averages would sooner or later catch up with us, and we would have to face tragedy.

Bradley was four months old when he was killed in a car accident. I remember the words that Rev. Frank Harrington first said when he came into Donna's home after Bradley's death: "This can make you or break you; the choice is yours." At the time I thought the words were harsh, but he was so right. We see ourselves either as victims of life or as students of life, and every experience good or bad can be used for growth and for good, but the choice is ours. It is fruitless to ask, "Why?" God never answers this question. But it is everything to ask, "How can I use this for God?" He always answers this question.

While we are never ready for this kind of loss, God's love was enough to get us through it. What follows is a letter I wrote to my family the Christmas after Bradley's death that started a chain reaction that has been a source of healing, not only for my family, but for others.

December 1983:

Christmas has a new meaning for me this year because of what has been happening in our family. I have had to rethink all of my understanding of who God is and what He does. I have always believed that tragedy and tribulation are part of living in an imperfect world, and not the will of a loving God. Now I am beginning to understand that material blessings are also a matter of chance and randomness, coupled with heredity, hard work, and intelligence. A loving God could not want some living in plenty while others starve.

I know that God the Creator created all things, but the one gift —the greatest gift—He offers to all is love. I know how much it cost God to see His son die and how much He loves me. God waits to pour this love into us, and through the power of the Holy Spirit empowers us to love as Jesus loves. Jesus' command to love one another and His command "Give and it will be given" are part of the same plan. For it is only when we love that we discover how many ways He can find to love us and how we discover who God is. This love is a free gift, or it is nothing, and to accept this gift and thus to be able to love is the only thing God depends on us to do. To accept love, to be able to love is the essence of faith.

When Bradley died and again when Jack (another grandchild) was so sick, many of our family and friends expressed their awareness and awe of our family being totally engulfed in love. I am now absolutely certain that, no matter what may happen to our family, God's love is enough to see us through.

Just before his death Jesus promised to send the Comforter: "I will not leave you desolate. I will come to you." Later, on the cross, he promised the thief, "This day you will be with me." To me, it follows that if Emmanuel means "God with us," then the spirit of those we love is also with us, very close and not somewhere "out there." Our temptation when hurt by tragedy is to withdraw into ourselves, but joy and healing come in the opposite direction when we claim Jesus' promises and reach out in love.

I can now say with Paul, "I have become absolutely convinced that neither death nor life, neither what happens tomorrow nor anything else in God's whole world, can separate us from the love of God in Christ Jesus our Lord" (Rom 8:37-39) and "when I think of the greatness of this plan I fall on my knees before the Father . . . and I pray that out of the glorious richness of His resources, He will enable you to know the strength of the Spirit's reinforcement—that Christ may actually live in your hearts by your faith, and I pray you, firmly fixed in love yourselves may be able to grasp . . . how wide and deep and long and high is the love of Christ—and to know for yourselves this love beyond our comprehension. May you be filled through all your being with God Himself" (Eph 3: 14-21).

That's the gift God gave each of us when Jesus was born. That's the gift each member of our family, past and present, gives to each other.

I love you,
Pappy

Bradley's death touched off a chain reaction that was remarkable. One thing that happened was that Dr. Harrington and I formed a close and lasting friendship from this tragic event.

Bo Bartlett was one of the students at Brookstone School whom I came to know through my children and my Sunday School class. When Bradley died, I commissioned Bo to do a painting of Mark 10:13-16, the verses Rev. Harrington used at Bradley's funeral service.

People were bringing little children to Jesus to have him touch them, but the disciples rebuked them. When Jesus saw this, he was indignant. He said to them, "Let the little children come to me, and do not hinder them, for the kingdom of God belongs to such as these. I tell you the truth, anyone who will not receive the kingdom of God like a little child will never enter it." And he took the children in his arms, put his hands on them and blessed them.

Bo Bartlett presented the painting to me, but refused payment. I have since learned that Bo's life had been deeply touched by the death of a brother. I'm sure that healing took place for Bo through the painting. He has now become a very famous and gifted artist. His painting hangs in the D. A. Turner Memorial Chapel at the W. C. Bradley Company. It is close to my office and is a source of great comfort to me and to others. Bo's letter to me about the painting follows.

Dear Mr. Turner,

The painting is entitled *Child with Christ*. It went through many changes from conception to completion. To achieve a simpler, more dynamic composition, I placed Christ and the child in the center. I changed the background many times, from blue sky to gray sky to rich forest green. I had to adjust the tonal value of the figures with each background change. The children began to encircle Christ as the painting developed. They seem to be part of a much larger crowd. They contain an active (coming, going, bustling, waiting) quality. The children are between the viewer and Christ. We would have to pass through them to meet him. This seems to suggest that symbolically we would have to go through them or be as little children, i.e. second innocence, to reach him.

I realized that this was a difficult subject when I agreed to paint it. When I began I could hardly bring myself to work on it. I was afraid that it would turn out like one of a hundred "silly" paintings of Jesus with children that I'd seen. I do celebrate life. That celebration sometimes appears obtuse because aesthetically I find it difficult to do "happy" paintings. Happiness is the most difficult of all the emotions to translate into serious art. Not that it is not a worthy state, but the tendency of Western culture is to perceive doom and gloom as the only worthy statements of "high art." The "decorative" or "popular" can acceptably portray happiness and joy.

My intention was to make a happy painting, but at the same time not lower my ideals for what I think art should aspire to. I struggled with the tone of the painting. I did not want it to get too dark, too serious, but the painting began to make me question. It dealt with topics that were extremely important to me, such as my own very real fatherly fear for the well-being of my own sons. I grew more emotionally charged as the painting progressed. I grew more anxious, more determined. There were times when I would work on it at night and get so frightened by the idea—this young child being picked up by Christ, Christ almost taking him "into" himself, absorbing—that it would become overpowering, and I would have to leave my brushes and ask my wife to clean off my palette for me. I could no longer be confronted with it.

The painting is strange; it is eery, oddly surreal, or supernatural. It refused, though, to be silly. It also refused to be happy on a superficial level.

Child with Christ not *Christ with Child.* He reaches toward the viewer, hand blurred in motion. Momentarily, he considers this realm. Half of the painting is saffron sky (heaven), and half is green (earth). Christ's body is enveloped by green as are the other children's, but his head is in the heavens, as is the child's he holds. The

136

colors are these: purple and green—the colors of thoughts, feelings, and emotions. Purple is the color of royalty (Godliness). Green is the color of life (of earthliness, of nature). White is like light (omniscience, silvery, his raiment—the uncolor, the all color of the spirit). And light blue, made from the combination of blue and white (the colors of Mother Mary, the colors of the cloud-covered earth from above, the color of air, of oxygen, of what sustains us) . . . The child that Christ holds close, that he is one with, is wrapped in light blue. His innocence is his only hope for attainment of breath. Of Pauch.

There are many things in this painting. They developed over many hours of working with it, struggling with it. My hope would be that one would meditate with it, allow it to unfold its meanings. A movement, a gesture, a stillness. Perhaps it is not a happy painting, but perhaps it reflects a deeper joy.

I've never before written to anyone my feelings on a painting, but I'll tell you the truth, no matter how accessible it may or may not be to others. There is something magical about this painting, magic in the highest sense. Because of all its placements and colors and meanings, its awkwardness and queerness, there remains something about it which is unutterable.

Bo Bartlett[10]

At the company's annual meeting in 1984 I made the presentation of the Bartlett painting. These were my remarks:

Child with Christ is the centerpiece of the Bradley collection because first and foremost the W. C. Bradley Company is a Christ-centered company, and we wish to acknowledge that our past and our future are built on Judeo-Christian values and that all we do comes from these values.

Second, the painting is the centerpiece because the company is a strongly family-oriented company, and we wish to dedicate this painting to all Bradley Company families who have experienced the loss of a child or who may in the future. We pray that this interpretation of Mark 10:13-16 will bring you comfort and hope.

Finally, this painting is our centerpiece because so much of the company's resources and energy go into the support of church and children. Our contributions go to churches, the Pastoral Institute, St.

Luke Early Childhood Development Center, Bradley Center Adolescent Hospital, Boys Club, Girls Club, Pediatric Unit of the Medical Center, Brookstone School, and Pacelli High School.

The next part of the chain reaction involves someone deeply touched by the painting. The letter, written in 1984, is to one of our co-workers, Jan Miller, from her sister Peggy who lost a child, Shannon, to leukemia. Since then she has had another child who had cancer. After long and painful treatment, this child has been miraculously healed. Peggy is a great inspiration to me and to all who know her.

Dear Jan:

I just received the statements. I meant to say letter, but I was so overwhelmed by the statements of Christ, by the artist, and Mr. Turner.

Truer interpretation could not have been made. Never before have I seen such a focal point of our lives and Shannon's placed in such a small, mysterious, and magnificent area as that field of canvas.

Christ's face is so real—not sad or in pain, but full of depth; not joyous, but so loving. That one child reminds me so much of Shannon and encourages me as to her placement in life with Jesus.

I praise God that this young man allowed himself to be touched by the Holy Spirit and paint what I feel is the closest reflection of Jesus and his relationship with us all that I have ever witnessed. Just as he said, it can be frightening, and we do want to turn away. But the fear is the desire to hold on to what we are and not venture into the unknown of what we can be with Christ.

I am so happy that you work for such a man as Mr. Turner. Truly he is one of God's disciples today, and his dedication and perseverance in an agnostic day and time are such encouragement for those of us who are weak in our conviction. Praise the Lord for Mr. Turner, praise the Lord for Bo, and praise the Lord for your mission: to carry out the dreams of the Lord through others—their talents (art), their hearts (caring) and their love (cohesiveness).

Love you and thank you,
Peggy[11]

The Gift of Resources

From my earliest recollection I had drilled into me the Parable of the Talents and the idea that "to whom much is given, much is required." But what really made the greatest impression on me was the quiet generosity of my grandfather and father, both of whom seemed to experience a great joy in giving without recognition. I remember when I received my first allowance—35 cents a week, a princely sum that would buy seven packages of chewing gum. I was told that I was expected to put 10 cents in the collection plate at church (two packages of gum). I was taught that we were supposed to tithe, but I wasn't taught the necessary math to convert my 35 cents into a tithe. Later, when I confronted my dad with this, he said, "Tithing is the minimum standard of giving, and it's done to remind us that all things belong to the Lord. You should ask the Lord what He wants you to do." While that lesson didn't sink in until much later, it did stay with me, and for years now my family and I have tried to give prayerfully. I don't feel boastful about this at all. It is my hope that everyone connected to our organization will feel a sense of ownership and joy in our philanthropic contributions because it is the fruit of their labor that gives us the wherewithal to give.

There is no doubt that our family has been financially blessed. My sisters and I, and now other family members, have tried to be good stewards through the foundations that my grandfather and father set up. My grandfather chartered the W. C. and Sarah H. Bradley Foundation on November 18, 1943, with 4,000 shares of W. C. Bradley Company Common Stock and some personal assets, and my father did the same on December 27, 1961, creating the D. A. and Elizabeth B. Turner Foundation. These foundations were merged in 1982 to become the Bradley-Turner Foundation.

The creation of the foundations was the beginning of servant leadership in our company, and I have tried to maintain and build on this tradition. I believe a servant leader should meet the needs of the people who work with him—at work, at home, and in the community. Through the foundation we have laid the groundwork to meet some of those needs.

Following the merger, my sisters and I started looking at how the Foundation was run. We'd been letting people come to us with their ideas, and we gave them money if we thought they had a good project. But we decided it was time we started looking at what the community needed and being proactive about it.

One of the most meaningful things we did was to create the Bradley Center to provide mental health services in Columbus. In the past, mental health was something not talked about much, and seeking help from a mental health professional tended to brand a person as "a little off" or even less charitably as "crazy" or "a nut case" and as a candidate for the "nuthouse." About the only places to go with emotional and behavioral problems was the state-run psychiatric hospital in Milledgeville, Georgia, or for those with the financial resources, a private psychiatric hospital in Atlanta. Columbus had one struggling psychiatrist who was unable to maintain his practice because of lack of community acceptance.

Once we made the decision to build a psychiatric hospital, the resources fell into place. I include my dad's close friendship with Dr. Norman Vincent Peale as one of those resources. The friendship between my dad and Dr. Peale was probably an example of a leap of faith. It began when my dad introduced himself to Dr. Peale one Sunday morning after attending his church service at Marble Collegiate Church in New York City. Dr. Peale was open and friendly, as was my dad, and they hit it off immediately.

Dr. Peale and his colleague, Dr. Smiley Blanton, had established the Institute of Religion and Psychiatry in New York City, and both were of great help to us in planning the Bradley Center. The Bradley Center opened on Second Avenue behind the YMCA building downtown in 1955 as an outpatient counseling center with a director, a psychiatric social worker, a psychologist, a minister, and a secretary. In 1958 it moved to a new 8-room building on Warren Williams Road. By 1968 funds were in place to build a 44-bed hospital at 1600 Sixteenth Avenue, near Lakebottom Park on property that had been the former site of the Anne Elizabeth Shepherd Home for Girls.

We were pleased that both Dr. Peale and Dr. Blanton came to Columbus for the opening ceremony for the hospital, and that Dr.

Peale returned for our 20th anniversary. Dr. Peale's book, *The Power of Positive Thinking*, and Dr. Blanton's book, *Love or Perish*, had much to do with shaping how the Bradley Center and our companies are managed.

As a result of their friendship, my father became a strong supporter of *Guidepost* magazine, which Dr. Peale and his wife started, and he bought subscriptions to it for all the teachers and ministers in this area. We have continued the practice since my father's death because of the very positive and appreciative response we get from the ministers, teachers, and stakeholders.

In celebration of its 20th anniversary, the Pastoral Institute recognized the Turner, Butler, and Corn families for their generous and unfailing support through the years by erecting a statue at its entrance. *Caring* is the work of nationally-known sculptor Marilyn Banks.

After the founding of the Bradley Center I was encouraged by Richard Robertson, a Methodist minister and a counselor at the center, to go to Calgary, Ontario, Canada, in 1974 to visit a pastoral counseling center there. Upon my return we created the Pastoral Institute, an outpatient counseling center that worked hand in hand with the Bradley Center hospital, and Richard became its first director.

In 1978 I heard an executive from General Motors speak in Columbus about a movement spreading across the country that I thought could be of value to the employees of the W. C. Bradley Company. It was called the Employee Assistance Program, and it provided drug and alcohol counseling services to employees as an employee benefit. Then the light came on for me that "Hey, it doesn't have to be limited to that. It can be for all of life's problems."

We introduced one of the first Employee Assistance Programs in Georgia to W. C. Bradley Company employees in 1978. At first it was threatening to a lot of people. Early on, people needed help badly if they took advantage of it. Now, that's not the case. People go for all sorts of reasons. CB&T, which is the lead bank in the Synovus family of companies, was the second company to join.

The Pastoral Institute, through its Business Resource Center, has continued to grow the Employee Assistance Program, and in 1999 contracts with 110 companies, offering mental health services to more than 50,000 employees plus their family members. It also led to the creation of an Affiliate Provider Network to provide counseling services to companies that have employees in other parts of the country. There is no doubt in my mind that the EAP is good business, but that ought not be the reason companies implement it. We did it because it's the right thing to do, because we care about our people—a living example of the Parable of the Mustard Seed!

Through expansion of services the Pastoral Institute has become more than a counseling center, though counseling remains its primary mission. Its Center for Education and Training offers community-wide life enrichment workshops, professional training for mental health and other professionals, and is an approved training facility for pastoral counselors nationally. Its Clergy Resource Center ministers to the needs of clergy through a Congregational Assistance Program that provides counseling services to congregations, support groups for local clergy, and a Clergy-in-Crisis Program for clergy and clergy families from across the nation.

The work of the Pastoral Institute does not go unnoticed. In 1994 the Pastoral Institute was named the Most Outstanding Pastoral

Counseling Center in the nation by the American Association of Pastoral Counselors.

In a number of ways the creation of the Bradley Center and the Pastoral Institute was an act of courage because of the stigma associated with mental illness, especially in the early years. But gradually that stigma has faded as people have come to understand and accept the idea of wellness for the whole person and the role the mind plays in the process.

When you get down to it, the reason mental health interested my sisters and me was that we saw a need for that kind of growth in our own lives and the freedom that came from it. I don't know that I have ever specifically said, "I'm going somewhere to get help," but through processing and learning and talking, I have gotten an awful lot of help. That place has been a blessing to me in my own personal growth.

I think that one of the obstacles that keeps people from getting the help they need is that they think of it as a weakness or a sickness. One of my goals has been to help people learn to grow and to look at it as a growth process. Everything we experience is part of the growth process. Pain is a part of growth, and we can help people deal with pain constructively. I think God gives us pain for the purpose of getting us to do something about it. I don't think we can grow without pain because growth involves change, and change is painful.

I have had many learning experiences through the Bradley Center and the Pastoral Institute that shaped my thinking on a number of topics, including servant leadership. Workshops by Viktor Frankl, who was a survivor of the Holocaust and the author of *Man's Search for Meaning*[12]; William Glasser, who wrote *Reality Therapy*[13]; Haim Ginott, author of *Between Parent and Child*[14]; and Virginia Satir, a noted mental health professional, author, and lecturer, taught me much about listening between the lines and meeting people's needs. Of course, Dr. Len Maholick and Dr. George Zubowicz, who were directors of the Bradley Center, were great coaches for me in my listening to young people.

Another way God has equipped us to empower others is through what the company and the foundation are doing in the community in the public/private partnerships we have formed and the proactive style of giving we have adopted to change the quality of life in our community. Through public/private partnerships, our city won the Women's Fast-Pitch Softball Olympic venue during the 1996 Summer Olympic Games and created a 15-mile Riverwalk, the new Columbus Civic Center, new recreation areas, and the Coca-Cola Space Science Center. The RiverCenter for the Performing Arts/the Columbus State University Schwob Department of Music is under construction. Columbus responded to our community challenge by raising $86.4 million to be used by nine organizations to improve the cultural and educational climate in Columbus. The funds raised by the Columbus Challenge is five times more than the best fund drive ever conducted in the city and is the largest campaign ever launched in the south and one of the largest in the nation.

A lifelong love of baseball inspired Bill as he threw out the first pitch at the Women's Fast Pitch Softball competition in Columbus during the 1996 Summer Olympics in which the U.S. won gold.

I've learned a number of lessons from the incredible public-private partnership experiences in Columbus. I believe these apply to most any relationship. For example,

• There is no limit to what we can do if we don't care who gets the credit.

• When we push power away, it empowers everyone, and we have even more power.

• When we listen and develop a common vision, everyone owns it.

- It is important to dwell on the positive because if you dwell on the negative, it will eventually kill the positive (in community, in business, in family). Even when you meet obstacles, you can find ways around them.

- We should find things to praise instead of blaming or making excuses because these are forms of self-justification, and self-justification is a form of self-worship, and this is always fatal.

- The solution to problems is not always found by the person behind the biggest desk.

- Response-ability is responding if we have the ability and not saying "that's not my job."

- We should be brave enough to live creatively. It is the only place no one has ever been.

I'm proud of what our city is accomplishing, but more importantly, I'm glad that its people share a sense of ownership for the great things that are happening here. I believe each person has the same needs that I do—a need for meaning in their lives, a need to feel that they are part of building a better world.

Someone asked me how I had been able to shift from performance-based self-esteem to service. I haven't completely. I still struggle with the same old childhood tapes telling me that worth comes from performance. In all honesty, service is the way I get self-esteem. I have to watch myself because I get self-esteem from being a rescuer, and that's not a good motivation for service or giving, but I hope one day I will be able to deny self and follow the Servant.

I don't want or need the acclaim that can come from giving, but I confess that at least part of my motivation to give comes from the good feelings I get, including the boost to my self-esteem. The Lord did say, "Give and it will be given unto you." I don't believe he was talking about giving us more money. I believe He meant the joy and humility that come from realizing and accepting that everything good comes from God and are gifts from Him to us, but He expects us to use those gifts wisely and to His glory.

Thoughts While Passing Through

- Those whom God calls, He equips.
- Don't let problems become excuses.
- Integrity doesn't mean honesty; it means completeness. Health doesn't mean the absence of disease; it means wholeness.
- Help me to remember that Jesus has other workers.
- Pain is a symptom that something is wrong.
- One reason miracles happen is because loving people will go to almost any length to keep people believing in miracles. Maybe that's the biggest miracle of all.
- If we love Christ, there must be a certain amount of pain. That's the way of the cross.
- If we bump someone, what is inside spills out. If you squeeze an orange, orange juice comes out because that's what's in it. If you put pressure on people, whatever is inside comes out—self-pity, anger, jealousy, or love.
- According to Mark 9:12, the mountaintop is for renewal, but the work is done in the valleys.
- It is impossible to hate someone when we pray for them.

All 21 grandchildren celebrated Pappy's 75th birthday, even though 3 attended via photos.

CHAPTER 8

FIRST, BE A SERVANT

All my life I have struggled to understand what it means to be great. The question of greatness led me to reflect on an incident found in Mark 10 where James and John asked Jesus for the choice places in his kingdom. Their request started a dispute about greatness among the disciples that provoked Jesus to reply, "He who would be great among you must be the servant of all." This same story is found in all of the synoptic Gospels with one major difference. Mark fingers James and John as the culprits who started the dispute. Luke, who was not one of the original disciples, blames all of the disciples for the dispute. Matthew acts like a man and blames a woman, the mother of James and John, for starting it. John who, according to Mark, was one of the guilty parties, doesn't even mention the incident in his Gospel, but he seems to have gotten the message better than all of the disciples.

If John had been a businessman, he probably would have pictured in his mind's eye a table of organization with God and Jesus at the top, then John in the next position with the whole world beneath him. After all, according to Genesis, God promised man dominion over all of His earth. Dominion means lordship, ownership, control, and power.

Relationships—with our Creator, our families, our friends, and others—are ultimately what is important in life. I believe we can destroy our relationships by focusing on the "Deadly Ps," but we can enrich them by embracing the "Christian Cs." The following chart includes questions I ask myself to keep me on track.

The Deadly Ps

Pride   Do you have a hard time admitting you are wrong? Do you have to win every argument? Do you blame others when things go wrong? Do you take credit for the good things that happen?

Prejudice   Are there people whom you look down on and think are inferior? Are there people whom you fear?

Position   Do you want the choice position at functions? Do you want to be recognized? Do you name-drop? Do you want to meet and be associated with famous people?

Popularity   Do you hold back your thoughts, flatter, or curry favor with people? Do you act in ways to seek approval from others or act in a different way with different crowds?

Possessions Do you judge yourself and other by their clothes, jewelry, cars, or houses? Do you try to possess people rather than serve them?

Power   Do you want to be in control? Do you try to use power to coerce others?

The Christian Cs

- *Commitment* produces caring.
- *Caring* produces compassion.
- *Compassion* produces communication.
- *Communication* produces creativity.
- *Creativity* produces common vision.
- *Common* vision produces community.

The following is a self-test I developed, based on 1 Corinthians 13, to keep myself on track. I believe this Scripture tells us how God wants us to live: with faith, hope, and love—the greatest of these being love. I try to apply these to my relationship with myself as well as my relationship with others because before I can effectively love others, I must love myself.

- *Love is patient*—Do you keep your cool when people disagree with you?

- *Love is kind*—Do you share your time and concern with others? Do you try to be thoughtful of those around you?

- *Love is not jealous*—Are you threatened by others' talents? Do you get upset when others are recognized for their performance?

- *Love is not conceited*—Do you focus attention on yourself or try to make yourself look good at the expense of others?

- *Love is not proud*—Do you know your limitations and ask for help when you need it?

- *Love is not ill-mannered*—Is your conversation polite and supportive, or do you put others down to make yourself look good?

- *Love is not irritable*—Are you touchy, defensive, or supersensitive? Or are you easy to approach?

- *Love keeps no record of wrongs*—Are you quick to forgive when someone hurts you?

- *Love is not happy with evil*—Do you delight when someone slips up or fails? Do you ignore evil unless it touches you?

- *Love is happy with truth*—Do you try to be an open, real person even when it shows your weakness? Are you willing to admit your mistakes?

- *Love never gives up*—Do you keep trying when someone rejects you? Do you continuously look for ways to love, care, and help?

It has taken me many years to understand this Scripture and many more to put it into practice in my life the way I believe the Lord intended. It has only been as I've grown in faith that I've come to understand that greatness never terminates in self and that it comes with loving service to all people in all areas of your life.

Most management schools have taught in the past that each business should have a table of organization that looks like this:

A Traditional View of Leaders

BOSS

MISSION
Please Boss by
Carrying Out
His Vision

In this model, which permeates not only businesses but the structure of families and almost all organizations, the boss is at the top with worker bees (employees) supporting the boss. Each worker bee must have a clear job description that outlines his/her responsibilities and authority, but the vision is always put in motion by the boss. The vision in most companies is to increase shareholder value—a worthy goal.

The problem is that in this traditional organization each worker responds to the boss. The organization is not flexible and is slow to deal with change. There is little room for creativity. Another problem is that the job does not offer fulfillment other than pay. The boss can reward performance with bonuses and recognition, but real fulfillment—the kind that reminds you of why you're on this planet—comes from outside the traditional organization.

Although traditional leadership has been the modus operandi for organizations, I am convinced that servant leadership will be the way to manage in the future, not only because it brings personal fulfillment to everyone in the organization, including the boss, but also because it can deal with change quickly and effectively.

Some people have become so used to an autocratic management style that they find it difficult to understand servant leadership and the benefits it offers. As I understood the old traditional management paradigm, the leader was at the top of the hierarchy, and many below wanted the position. Driven by ego to seek position and power, they managed by coercion. This caused them to claim credit for things that went well and to blame others when things went wrong. My experience with being at the top of the traditional organization was that it was a very lonely position. When people were nice to me, I never knew if they really liked me, whether they thought I was omnipotent, or if they were just seeking favor to enhance their own position. I felt my major responsibility was to motivate and manage (manipulate) those who were doing the tasks. Everyone's focus in this kind of organization is on pleasing the leader. I can remember raising havoc once because inventories were too high. The results of my "management" was that inventories were drastically reduced, but so were sales. We didn't have a "full wagon" of goods to sell.

The servant leader organization looks differently:

Servant Leadership Model

Based on the tenant that servant leadership is a commitment to love and serve, the organizational structure is turned upside down, with the leader at the bottom of the hierarchy, supporting those who do the work. The leader's primary responsibility is to meet the needs, whatever they may be, of those who serve the organization. It involves listening to others and together shaping a vision that everyone can own. The servant leader becomes a funnel that creative ideas come to naturally from others who are themselves becoming servant leaders. Servant leaders are encouragers, communicators, and cheerleaders.

Servant leadership is more than just a way to run a business. One definition I've heard for a servant leader is someone who has the ability not to sit back and watch the world go to hell. Teddy Roosevelt once said the world will not be a great place to live until it is a good place for all of us to live. Servant leadership is bigger than an institution. It must include a sense of responsibility for community inside and outside the institution, as well as for the stakeholders.

In the traditional organization the tendency is to point fingers. In a servant leader organization it is to raise hands. In the traditional organization the tendency is to say "It's not my responsibility." In the servant leader organization it is to say "Here I am. Send me."

Servant leaders never take credit for creativity and success, blame others for failure, or stifle creativity by saying "That's been tried before," or worse, "That's never been tried." The servant leader never ignores ideas. Lack of response drives creative people up the wall. Tactfully turning down a creative person doesn't stop creativity. The creative person is already thinking of a better way or a way around your objection. Servant leaders never express negative thoughts because they know that negativity kills positive thoughts every time.

The beginning point of servant leadership may be the humility of knowing yourself. This is hard for me to do unless I constantly remind myself that even though I may be a mess, God loves me just as I am and that He is calling me to be what He wants me to be.

When I assume the mantle of a servant leader, I also assume the responsibility to help people grow, and if I am to succeed in doing this, I must give up control. I am just beginning to understand and give up my prior bias that a leader must be in control. I have had to let go of most of my titles to do this. But it is an atmosphere of love and caring that enables the "reborn" leader to turn the traditional organization upside down so that all who belong to the organization can experience the same self-discovery and the freedom to be and become. Under this type of organization the people at Char-Broil who put the grill in the box become as important as anyone else in the organization. The leader cannot ask for the commitment of others unless they themselves are fully committed. Love is a commitment to extend oneself for others, and the feeling follows the behavior. The leader creates the climate and is constantly asking, "Are people growing, becoming more trusting and spirit-filled, becoming servants? Is there more creativity, more energy and enthusiasm, and more hope?" If not, another dose of humility may be in order.

I heard David Whyte, author of *The Heart Aroused*,[15] say that "the antidote for exhaustion is not necessarily rest, but is wholeheartedness." I believe that this may be the source of much of the energy for servant leadership. I fully believe that this is what Jesus meant when he said, "Love one another . . . I have told you these things so that my joy might be in you and your joy might be complete" (John 15:11). This is the "living water" that never runs dry, and there are many who are searching for it.

A servant leader, to borrow a phrase from Rotary, puts service above self. In his book *Leadership Is an Art*,[16] Max DePree writes:

> The best people working for organizations are like volunteers . . . They choose to work somewhere for reasons less tangible than salary or position. Volunteers don't need contracts; they need covenants . . . Covenant relationships rest on shared commitments to ideas, to issues, to values, to goals, and to the management process.

DePree adds that "covenant relationships induce freedoms." This freedom includes the freedom to dream and communicate your dream to others, and this enables the people in a covenant relationship with an organization to put their dreams together to meet common needs and to build common visions. This freedom includes the freedom to risk and to trust and to love.

Servant leadership is a circle of love in which a commitment to caring produces compassion that, in turn, produces communication, creativity, and common vision—which ultimately produce a caring community.

The W. C. Bradley Company Museum and the D. A. Turner Memorial Chapel are excellent examples of how this works. The vision for the museum began when I asked some of the key players in our stakeholders department, together with certain key shareholders, to brainstorm about what would be the most creative way to celebrate the company's 100th anniversary in 1985. We were looking for something other than the usual dinner with speeches that other old companies had. What we were doing was listening to each other and developing a common vision everyone could own.

Bill Turner often goes to the D. A. Turner Memorial Chapel, just a few steps from his office, to reflect. The chapel was a gift to the company from its employees in honor of "Mr. D. A." and in recognition of the company's 100th anniversary. (Photo by Mike Culpepper Studios)

While I'm sure that the idea for a museum came from someone there, it is the process that created the vision that is important, and to single out one person would be to defeat the process. We had some people on the committee who had demonstrated a keen interest and knowledge of art. This group, led by Susan Wiggins, vice-president of our stakeholders department, and made up of Betty Corn, Jan Miller, and Elizabeth Ogie, requested various art museums throughout the country to send a list of budding artists we might consider. From this list and from samples of their work, we selected the artists we wished and instructed them to "paint the W. C. Bradley Company." When their work was finished, we held an open house for all W. C. Bradley

Company team members and the community. What I didn't know at that time was that a group of W. C. Bradley Company team members was collecting funds to build a chapel honoring my father. What an appropriate, kind, generous, and thoughtful gesture on their part! Nothing could have pleased Dad more. In addition to being used for devotionals and Bible studies, the chapel and the museum are often the scene of christenings and weddings for our W. C. Bradley Company family and friends.

As time went on, we realized that the museum would not be as relevant to new employees as it is for the older ones because of changes in the company and because of death. We began the annual Spirit Award initiative in 1990 to solve this problem. Each year we ask everyone in the company to nominate their fellow workers who best exemplify the spirit and values of our company. The criteria for selection includes spiritual values and family values, as well as relationships with fellow workers, vendors, church, community, and customers. From these nominations a committee selects five or six winners to have their portrait painted by Garry Pound, a wonderfully talented local artist. These paintings hang in our museum for a year and then are given to the recipients of the Spirit Awards, and we replace these paintings with a new group. The Spirit Award ceremony and the paintings not only keep our museum new and fresh, but also creates a sense of ownership among all the W. C. Bradley Company family and also reminds each of us of our heritage and the values we build upon. And of course, its location in the old W. C. Bradley Company cotton warehouse keeps us in touch with our roots. A museum is a living thing, and it is important that we keep it alive, fresh, and new for those who follow us.

As chairman of the company, I could have blocked the funnel's flow of energy and creativity in a number of ways, and we might have ended up with a traditional dinner. But I didn't, and our team created a unique way to celebrate our birthday.

One of our managers asked, "What do you do when an employee in an organization tries to sabotage servant leadership?" The answer is simple. I love him, coach him, and try to understand his behavior. But I know that there may come a time, if he is in a position that blocks the growth of others, that he may have to be removed. I ask myself,

"What is the loving thing to do?" Sometimes removing the person is the loving thing. My caring doesn't have to end there, though. God created each of us, and I owe it to the person to try to help him find his place in God's plan.

Since my retirement from the companies I have done a lot of reflecting about servant leadership and where this attitude came from in our company. We tend to ignore or push down the parts of our story that we are not ready to claim or believe. I have revisited the early examples set by my grandfather and father. I always saw these men and other leaders I admired as men of power, and I saw them in control of their people and their enterprises. I missed the examples of servant-hood they set. I see now that my grandfather and my father both laid a firm foundation on which to build a servant company. My dad was a forerunner of what servant leadership is all about.

His father was Bill Turner's model of a servant leader. Mr. D. A.'s portrait in Bill's office serves as a daily reminder of the values he taught. (Photo by Mike Culpepper Studios)

Once in his last years my dad said, "I've tried to be a caretaker until you took over." Because of his lack of a college education, he felt that he was not equipped to manage a large company, so he developed the habit of listening to everyone who worked with us. He was a caretaker with the emphasis on caring, and this came through loud and clear for all who worked with him. He was a caretaker in the sense that he also preserved and nurtured the values of the company.

One of the good things about higher education is that you learn that while a college education helps, it does not equip you for leadership. My plan on graduation was to pursue an MBA, but the war intervened and I never went back. That was probably a good thing for me because, when I did take over the company, I followed the style of my dad and did an awful lot of listening and walking around. If he hadn't been my example, I might well have been running a company with a different set of values.

My reflections also showed me that when my minister asked me to teach Sunday School, and I replied that I wasn't equipped spiritually, intellectually, or morally, his call was a clear call to ministry. And his response to my disclaimer, "Be real; and when talking about Jesus, tell only what you know and know that you know," was a clear call to a leap of faith. I studied the Bible and learned about Jesus, but I had a tendency to ignore the parts of Jesus' teaching that didn't fit my image of what a leader should be. I'm sure there are leaders who follow a conventional table of organization who don't fall into this trap, but I did because I chose to ignore the clear message the Bible gives us.

I also should have grasped servanthood when I was part of the team that nursed, bathed, and took care of Tex Rhoden after his operation. Even though I felt this was something God wanted me to do or be, I missed "the greatest shall be a servant of all," and I missed how my being a servant enabled Tex to become a servant.

I was pointed toward servant leadership when I began my search for meaning in my life. I realized that if I needed meaning, other people might have the same need. There are two simple illustrations that show what I mean.

Bishop Ernest Fitzgerald tells the story of a young man entering a country store and when he didn't see Henry, the handyman, in his usual place asleep on the feed sacks, he asked the owner, "Where's Henry?" The owner replied "Henry died." With this, the young man, brightening up because he was looking for a job, said, "I guess that means you have a vacancy." The owner replied, "Nope. Henry didn't leave no vacancy." Each of us wants to believe our life makes a difference.

The second illustration was a poster in my Sunday School room that showed a teenager sitting on a curb alone. The caption read, "Out of my loneliness I will fashion a song, and when I find someone who hears my song, we will sing it together."

These two illustrations are the pulse of servant leadership. Listening, hearing, understanding, healing, building community, and discovering meaning will cause people to change and to grow, which is the goal of a servant leader.

Servant leadership must be grounded in a love that is a spiritual gift. And it must reach outside the organization in many ways to create a caring community and ultimately to build a better world. In a servant-led organization, the basis for all decision making should be, "What is the loving thing to do?"

There is a deep spiritual hunger in all of us to find a place where people really care for one another, where we can find something to believe in and something and someone to trust. When these things are discovered together in community, great things can happen. Believing in the worth and goodness of people is basic to servant leadership. I can either take a stance reaching out to others or a stance defending my position. There is far less danger in reaching out than there is to grasping and holding.

Kahlil Gibran in *The Prophet*[17] has someone tell the Prophet: "Speak to me of work." The Prophet replies, "Build your house as if your beloved will live there." The goal of servant leadership is to build a place where everyone is loved, a caring community.

What is a caring community? I think a caring community can be any relationship of love. It can exist in a church, a school, a small group, or a family. I envision it as a circle of love with three doors, one door representing self, one representing others, and one representing God, with the key to all of these doors being acceptance. Jerry Kramer, the perennial all-pro guard with the Green Bay Packers professional football team, was once asked "What is the secret of the Packers' greatness?" Kramer could have replied, "We have the greatest coach in the world"—which was true—or "We have the finest players," or "We are the best conditioned team," but he didn't say any of these things. He replied very quietly, very simply, and yet beautifully and profoundly, "We love each other."

I believe that what happens in a caring community is not only a part of, but also proves the validity of the Christian experience. I believe this because I have seen it happen a number of times with people in different age groups. I have seen people's lives literally transformed when they accepted the fact that they were accepted. I have seen young people ask for a Bible study course because, once they accept their acceptance and see the validity of Jesus' teaching, they learn that the Bible is not a stuffy, moldy old book but is really the story of the love that waits. They learn that the Ten Commandments and the Sermon on the Mount are not hard rules to prevent them from having a good time, but are literally road maps given by a loving God to see that their lives don't end up on a dead-end street.

When a person enters a caring community, he experiences a new acceptance, based not on how he looks or how he acts, but because he is. These new feelings of self-worth stimulate within him the desire to communicate. Parenthetically, I would also say that anything that destroys a person's self-worth also destroys any opportunity for real communication. Every day we make killer statements to each other that totally block any chance of our discovering who we are.

Jesus used this technique of accepting people as they are in all of his relationships. With the woman at the well he did not condemn her because she was a prostitute, but because he cared and accepted her, he stimulated within her the desire to be the person that he saw she could be.

A caring community stimulates a new kind of learning and growth typified by a new kind of three R's: risk, responsibility, and reality. As a person experiences self-worth, he risks taking an honest look at himself and his true feelings. We have been taught since childhood to hide our hate, our pains, our frustrations, and our suffering. We will do anything to escape the reality of these feelings, by any means—drugs, alcohol, or television. When we refuse to look at our feelings, we rob ourselves of an opportunity to grow and to change. This is why I think Jesus said, "You must come as a little child." I believe we need to unlearn many of these habits we have learned since childhood. Friedrich Nietzsche said, "When you have a 'why' to suffer, you can survive any 'how.' " Our own growth and learning to understand each other's suffering are reasons enough to endure any suffering that comes our way.

The second thing that happens in a caring community is that we begin to accept full responsibility for our own behavior. So much of our time and energy is wasted on self-pity and in making statements such as "I could be different if . . ." rather than accepting full responsibility, admitting the situation we are in and that we have many choices of how we can react to any given situation.

The third thing that happens when a person experiences self-worth in a caring community is that he is willing for the first time to face reality. As a person experiences his own unique personhood and is willing to take a good hard look at his own "phoniness," he sees how often he conforms to the situation in which the world places him. I commend young people for their desire to establish their own individuality and to escape from conformity. Yet I feel that I must warn them that a pair of blue jeans can be just as much of a trap as a Brooks Brothers suit, and I am afraid that some of the time what they are really saying is, "I want to be different, like everybody else."

When one of my children was small, he brought home a story that is so corny that I apologize before I tell it, but I think it illustrates perfectly the kind of dilemma we sometimes find ourselves in. This young boy was hell bent and determined to be his own person, to be an individual. He did not want his hair to be like his father's, which was short, or like his friends', which was long, so to be different he decided to part his hair from ear to ear. But he had to change because everyone kept trying to whisper to his nose. People just won't let us be our true selves. This is why Paul admonishes us, "Don't let the world about you squeeze you into its mold, but let God remold your mind from within so that you may prove in practice that God's plan for you is good, meets all of His demands, and leads to true maturity."

To experience love, a person must risk being vulnerable and transparent to others. When he does this, he will discover an even greater love, and he will also experience a reciprocal openness and honesty on the part of others. We begin to minister to the little child who exists in all of us because all of us have a great need, not only to be caring, but also to be cared for.

There are many byproducts that come from a life in a caring community. In my opinion our forefathers did us a great disservice when they wrote about pursuit of happiness, freedom, and peace of mind. These are things that can't be pursued, but are things that come naturally when a person experiences his own self-worth and faces the reality of his own situation. We find that we begin to develop an orderly value system that prevents us from being pulled in all directions as we try to make choices. We find that our goals in life take on more meaning and purpose.

I received a letter from a young man I had in Sunday School. This boy had everything—looks, intelligence, personality—but he was an agnostic who only came to Sunday School because his parents made him, and I never got through to him.

He wrote me recently, after having been in an encounter group, and what he said was this: "I have discovered that I can reach all of the goals I set for myself in life. I can make it with the girls. I can attain wealth, position, recognition, and fame. But it is not enough. It all adds up to a big zero. I'll be home in two weeks, and I want to talk to you." This is the kind of thing that happens when a person really begins to take an honest look at himself, his values, and his goals.

Another byproduct of being in a caring community is the freedom to fail. There is a wonderful story in the Bible about David that I don't believe I have ever heard a sermon about. I don't know why, because it has a message all of us need to hear. David was one of the first successful teenagers. He knocked off the champ, he had great success with girls, he had wealth, recognition, and even was made a king. But somewhere along the line he began to feel that he alone was responsible for his success. He forgot all about God, and he forgot to obey God's commandments. David was overtaken by great emptiness, loneliness, and depression. If you ever get to feeling this way, read some of the psalms David wrote during his period of separation from God, and you'll discover what loneliness and suffering really mean.

In one particular story David's wife was looking out the window one day. (I don't know why, but when I read the story I imagine David's wife looking like Flip Wilson dressed up as Geraldine.) David's wife saw a strange sight. David was in the courtyard in front of the Ark of the Covenant, and he was dancing all over the place.

From the story in the Bible he had on a short mini skirt with nothing under it, and his wife's handmaidens were sitting around with their mouths wide open and their eyes popping out. David's wife hollered out the window, "David, come in the house this minute." He hollered back, "I can't." She hollered back, "David, you are making a complete fool of yourself. Come into the house." David hollered back, "I can't stop dancing. I have just discovered that God still cares for me in spite of all I have done, and He still has a place for me in His plan." David had discovered that when we're at our worst, that is when God is at His best, for He never stops caring—no matter how we fail Him!

The most important thing a person will discover when he enters a circle of love or caring community is that eventually he will discover God. A Catholic priest, Father Louis Evely, has written a wonderful little book called *Our Prayer* in which he says, "You will never know any other God than the one you become . . . you will never know love except by loving . . . for it is through the love that we feel for another person (even a person who is unlovely) that you first know the wonder of the love that God has for you."

Christopher Morley once wrote that if we were given a five-minute warning that the world was coming to an end, every telephone in the country would be occupied with people trying to tell others that they love them. We don't have to wait for the world to come to an end. I firmly believe that our entire world can be a caring community provided we accept the fact that we are accepted; provided we keep loving ourselves and others; provided we keep risking, keep breaking out, keep growing, and keep dancing.

There's a very old bit of Chinese logic that says if you place two men on opposite sides of a mountain and they start digging toward each other and meet, you will have a tunnel through the mountain, but if they don't meet, you will have two tunnels. For nearly 2000 years Christian theologians have been digging away at the mountain of human indifference with the message that the greatest task assigned to man is to love God, not because God is some jealous, neurotic being, but because the love of God leads ultimately to love of self and to love of others. For the most part, the tools used by these theologians have been the reading and the hearing of God's word. More recently psychologists began on the opposite side of the same mountain digging away with the message that love of self is a vital ingredient of personal growth and self-actualization and that the more we can accept and understand ourselves, the more we can accept, understand, and care for others. They also contend that where such a caring community exists, personal growth and development take place in the same way that warmth allows a baby chick to break out of its shell and grow. The embryo of a baby chick can exist indefinitely inside the prison of its shell, but there is something about the warmth that makes it wish to come alive and to risk and to break out and to reach its full potential. The motivation for psychologists to dig their tunnel has been the persistent belief in the dignity, value, and potential of each individual.

Wouldn't it be something if the tunnels theologians are digging and the tunnels the behavioral scientists are digging met in the middle of our mountain of human indifference? Wouldn't it be something if the message Jesus was living and teaching 2,000 years ago when he offered us the keys to a rich and abundant life was the same formula being offered by psychologists? Wouldn't it be something if the first-century church with its emphasis on the Kingdom of God being a kingdom of right relationships—of self with self, of self with others, and of self with God—was the same kind of caring community? And wouldn't it be something if we could have this Kingdom of God right now?

I've often wondered how we'll know if our company is becoming a servant leader organization. I think the following example helps erase the doubt. On their own, our employees started an e-mail daily devotional. This devotional is printed out for those who don't have access to a computer. In February 1999 this e-mail was received:

To: Daily Devotional
From: Tommy Leak
Subject: Urgent Need for Your Prayers

Sue Jackson's (Corp HR) daughter, Jandee Cain, is in a hospital near Atlanta where she lives. Jandee has had a very difficult pregnancy. Due to severe complications, Jandee was admitted to the hospital about two weeks ago, and the baby had to be taken prematurely. Janna Makaylee Cain was born on Tuesday, 2/23/99, weighing just 1 lb. 5 oz. Baby and mama are in critical condition. Unfortunately, Jandee's condition has not improved since the baby was born and seems to have gotten worse.

Please take a moment, find someplace quiet, and lift Jandee, baby Janna, and father Johnny up in prayer. Nothing in this life is more important than how we care for each other. Time is critical, and these people urgently need your prayers. If things are going to improve, God will need to set things in motion. May God bless you all.[18]

Along with Tommy's message was an address where people could write, and our team members responded to the call with words of love and encouragement.

On March 1 Tommy again e-mailed the Daily Devotional to give everyone an update on the situation. His message read:

Please take a moment and praise God for hearing our prayers! Over the last three days Jandee has gotten much better. In fact, the doctor let her go home yesterday. She is still having to monitor her blood pressure hourly and is still taking quite a bit of medication, but she is home and is sure to recuperate faster there.

Baby Janna has been nicknamed "Firecracker" by the hospital staff. She is a fighter, and the doctors have been pleased by her progress. They have moved her to an incubator, which is considered a step forward. Soon they hope to remove the breathing machine and allow her to breathe on her own. Doctors do point out that the second week of life is more difficult for premature babies. Sue said they are just taking it one day at a time.

Please continue to pray for Janna, Jandee, and Johnny. Baby Janna has a long fight ahead of her and really needs your continued prayers. If all goes well, it will still be another three months before baby Janna will be able to go home.

Thank you so much for your prayers. I will keep you posted of their status. May God richly bless each of you and your families.[19]

This is what I hoped would happen in a servant leader organization —a deep caring based on the presence of God in our lives, grounded in prayer. The little "Firecracker" was later taken off the respirator and was breastfeeding, though she still was not out of the woods. I am reminded of another letter I received once from one of our team members who had lost a child. In it she said, "The beauty of our company is that when one person cries, everyone tastes the tears."

When Lee Lee James called me on my car phone on December 21, 1998, to tell me the news that *Fortune* magazine had selected Synovus as the best place to work in the country, I was so excited that I pulled off the road to reflect on what that really meant.

My first reaction was one of gratitude, pride, and fulfillment. Three generations in my family had laid the foundation that made this possible, but we didn't deserve the credit for making it happen unless we created an atmosphere that attracted hundreds of people who made it happen. At least we didn't get in their way. The marvelous thing about the Synovus celebration was that everyone felt part of the team that had created the best-place attitude.

My second reaction was, "Where do we go from here? What do we do for an encore?" After being selected number one, anything else would be anti-climactic, and it stands to reason that *Fortune* will pick someone else next year. But being number one on someone else's list is really not all that important. It's how you feel in your heart that is important.

My third reaction was that there have to be places in our company where people don't agree that Synovus is the best place to work. We must make a special effort to identify these places and correct them, or they will eventually spread like a cancer throughout the company because negative attitudes overwhelm positive ones every time.

My last reaction was, "How do we stay humble with all of the accolades Synovus is getting?" I am reluctant to write about humility because I believe that when you think you have it, you've lost it. But because of the great success and accolades our companies and our people have received, I am concerned that we might lose our humility. I've tried several things to counteract the loss of humility.

First, it's difficult to be anything but humble before God, especially if you pray whatever prayer is in your heart. I've found that the most effective prayer is what's in your heart, whether it's anger, guilt, jealousy, pride, grief, or joy. A second way to retain humility, I think, is the study of the life of Jesus and his example and teachings on servanthood. I always feel humble when I read the Sermon on the Mount (Matt 5–7) or 1 Corinthians 13. And it's impossible for me not to be humble when I remember the cross. I carry a cross in my pocket to remind me of what Jesus did for me and why he did it. Third, Sue Marie always keeps my feet on the ground.

In 1998, right after Synovus received the honor, my son Brad wrote me a beautiful letter that I will always treasure. It is important to me for many reasons, but especially because it shows love and sensitivity to my needs and because it shows he has a clear vision of what is at the base of our company's success:

Dad,

Not that you are looking for any strokes, but I could not help but think as I celebrate Synovus' recognition that initiatives like the Bradley Center, the Pastoral Institute, the EAP, St. Luke Childhood Development Center, Prayer Breakfast, etc. came from you and came a long time ago before *Fortune* started recognizing such benefits to employees. What we have taken for granted around here because of you, the rest of the country is now starting to applaud as valuable.

You are and have always been a great standard-bearer that a results-oriented culture and a people-oriented culture are not in conflict. CB&T, Synovus/TSYS, and WCB have all been the beneficiaries of this—your wonderful legacy.

Love,
Brad[20]

I appreciated Brad giving me credit for what is happening, but I'm getting a clearer vision of the real cause as I understand it. Like the Green Bay Packers, we too have the best coaches and players, but it's because we care deeply for each other that we were selected number one. And if we continue to love each other, we'll stay number one regardless of whose list we're on or not on because "love outlasts everything" (1 Cor 13:8), and love is a gift from God.

I have found examples of servanthood in the most unlikely places. Each year at Halloween the children from the child development center at St. Luke United Methodist Church dress in their costumes and visit our offices. Very little work gets done until after the children leave because everyone is busy decorating themselves and their offices in preparation for the children's visit. After the children arrive, they line up to get their "treats" from people along the way. This year I didn't realize the number of children at the child development center had doubled, and I was running perilously close to having an empty basket with many "goblins" still in line. Finally I was down to three pieces of candy, with five children still to go, when a little "Tinkerbell" stopped in front of me, stared into my basket, then looked at her basket overflowing with candy, and then looked at the line behind her. She reached down and scooped several handfuls of candy into my basket before moving along. That is a perfect example of the essence, and attitude, of servant leadership.

I think Teilhard de Chardin may have had servant leadership in mind when he wrote "Someday after we have mastered the wind, the waves, the tides, and gravity, we shall harness for God the energies of love, and then for the second time in the history of the world, man will have discovered fire."

Thoughts While Passing Through

- If it takes experience to strengthen our faith, experience can also weaken our faith.
- If I can will myself to love someone who is unlovely, can I will myself to love myself? And can I will myself to surrender and allow God's love to fill me and overflow to others?

- The only questions worth asking God can be answered by faith. Saying Christianity is a set of beliefs is like saying marriage is a set of beliefs.
- People wonder why people do bad things. It would be more productive to wonder why they do good things.
- When we have small dreams or a small vision, we accomplish small things.
- If we are too preoccupied with the future, we lose the opportunities of the present. But if we don't have faith in the future, we won't have power in the present. The Kingdom of God is now.
- It is impossible to obey God without the empowerment of the Holy Spirit.

Four generations: D. A. Turner, Little Bill Turner, Brad Turner, Bill Turner

CHAPTER 9

THE VIEW FROM WHERE I SIT —THE LEGACY

Teach me, O Lord, not to hold onto life too tightly. Teach me to hold it lightly, not carelessly, but lightly, easily. Teach me to take it as a gift to enjoy and to cherish while I have it and to let it go gracefully and thankfully when the time comes. The gift is great, but the Giver is greater still. Thou, O God, are the Giver, and in thee is the life that never dies.[21]

—Theodore Parker Ferris

Someone reading the title of this chapter might have visions of an old man sitting in a rocking chair, shawl around his shoulders, waiting for the inevitable, gazing out the window at a bleak and uninteresting landscape. That is not what I see. From where I sit, the view is lovely, and part of that view is seeing the complete and incomplete tapestry of my life in a way that makes Romans 8:28 exciting and true.

In one of her poems Dawna Markova speaks to me when she writes, "I will not die an unlived life." I have tried to live fully every moment of my life. I think that in order to live well, we also have to come to terms with death, which is as much a part of life as birth. There is tremendous freedom and joy in doing this when coupled with the Christian faith.

Someone asked me to explain how I came to develop my philosophy (theology) of leadership. I can now see that all of my experiences, good and bad, have shaped who I am:

- my Christian home

- my time at sea where the possibility of death became a reality for a young man who saw himself as immortal and forever young, who out of sheer boredom read Will Durant's *Story of Philosophy* and began a quest for truth that has never ended

- my teaching Sunday School 50-plus years and all that I've learned while teaching

- my marriage and the love and reality it brought into my life

- my time of emptiness that caused me to attend the Laymen's Leadership Institute where I met Christian businessmen who had found their ministry and mission

- my involvement with the Lay Witness Movement and Faith at Work, particularly colored by the lectures of Father John Powell

- the establishment of the Bradley Center and the Pastoral Institute and the realization that many of our clients were there because their lives were empty

- my listening to Viktor Frankl lecture at the Bradley Center and reading his book, *Man's Search for Meaning*

- the experience of tragedy and realizing that God's love is enough

These are examples of a list that could be endless, all a part of an unfinished tapestry.

I suppose I could coast the rest of my life. Many people do. They seem to reach a point where they say, "I've worked hard, done much. Now I'm going to sit back and enjoy it in the time I have left." I have no problem with this, if that's what makes them happy. But it seems to me that unless we "retire from in order to retire to," we will lose interest in life pretty soon or, as my dad put it, "We will rust out long before we wear out." I'm sure my feelings are colored by my old "tapes" that play "Your worth is based on your performance." But it also seems that everything that ever happened to me is preparing me for what lies ahead, and there is a sense of urgency to get on with God's vision for me. I want to use well the time I have left. Each day is an opportunity for joy, and I have no intention of just sitting and rocking. There's just so much to do! This is exciting and fun, and I can hardly wait for tomorrow to come. Each day is a new adventure. I will leave this world when the tapestry is completed, when I have completed the mission(s) God had in mind for me when He created me.

I suppose I've done enough in my life to supply the minister with a decent "résumé" to read when my time comes. Sometimes at funerals I get the impression that the minister is trying to say enough nice things about the deceased to get them into heaven. There have been times when I wanted to look in the casket to be sure I was at the right funeral.

I want none of this at my celebration of life. The decision whether I make it to heaven has already been decided before I draw my last breath. I want the minister to concentrate on God's gift of love, as expressed in Romans 8:26-28 and John 14:15-18 (the covenant Jesus made to us and the covenant I make to all I love). I want him to read three things I keep in my Bible that kids in my Sunday School class have given me:

> Hours fly,
> Flowers die,
> New days,
> New ways,
> Pass by.
> Love stays.

> Time is
> Too Slow for those who Wait,
> Too Swift for those who Fear,
> Too Long for those who Grieve,
> Too Short for those who Rejoice;
> But for those who Love,
> Time is not.
> —Henry Van Dyke[22]

Where there is faith,
There is love.
Where there is love,
There is peace.
Where there is peace,
There are blessings.
Where there are blessings,
There is God.
Where there is God,
Nothing is wanting.

—Slovak house blessing

When I die, give what is left of me to children.
If you need to cry, cry for your brothers working beside you.
Put your arms around anyone, and give them what you need to give me.
I want to leave you with something, something better than words or sounds.
Look for me in the people I have known and loved.
And if you cannot live without me,
Then let me live on in your eyes, your mind, and your acts of kindness.
You can love me most by letting hands touch hands and letting go of children who need to be free.
Love does not die; people do.
So when all that is left of me is love, give me away.[23]

— Merrit Malloy

Even though I'm in the autumn of my years, I remain focused on the future, and while I have a vision for what I want that to be like, it's more important that members of my family (in all its forms—birth, company, church, and community) have their own common vision of what they wish to see happen. This vision should come after much dreaming, sharing, and listening, really listening to each other's dreams so that their common vision meets everyone's needs. It would be my hope that the new vision will be built on the foundation that has been left for them.

I read that the first mayor of the Plymouth colony was impeached four years after the colony's founding because he built a road five miles into the wilderness. He had a vision of the colony growing as others sought refuge in a free world, but he made the fatal mistake of not taking the time to sell the vision to others in a way that would cause them to embrace it. These were people who had shared the common vision to cross a vast ocean at great risk in order to be free, but because they did not own the new vision, it failed. A vision is a dynamic thing and must be nurtured, or it will die. When we reach a goal, we must raise the bar, or we risk losing the vision.

It is my hope that my "family" will build on the foundation that is here, and that they will dream great dreams because no one ever got excited about small dreams. If we continue to dream great dreams, we will continue to accomplish great things.

Thoughts While Passing Through

- If Christ hadn't been wounded, I wouldn't feel forgiven or loved. If I hadn't been wounded, could I listen and understand? Don't let pain be in vain.
- Death is a challenge not to waste time. Show someone you love them right now.
- One of the beauties of age is that you can view life from the crest of the hill. When you look back over life, if you've lived it well, you are looking from high ground and can see where God has led you through rough ground, through thickets and swamps, in good weather and bad, leading you back to the right path that leads to even higher ground.
- Whoever said money can't buy happiness never took ten grand-children to Disney's World on Ice or bought a little granddaughter her first ice cream cone or puppy.
- Peace is more than the absence of violence. It is the spirit of recon-ciliation, the presence of community, the joy of giving, and the power of love.

[1] Adapted, "Epistle Dictionary," *Man and Superman* (New York: Dodd, Mead, and Co., 1947) 510.

[2] Translated by Paul Burns (New York: Herder and Herder, 1970).

[3] Used by permission of author.

[4] *The Shoes of a Fisherman* (London: The Reprint Society, 1963). Used by permission of author.

[5] New York: Washington Square Press, 1965.

[6] Chicago: Argus Communications, 1969.

[7] New York: Simon and Schuster, 1978.

[8] New York: Macmillan, 1962.

[9] "Hast Thou No Scars?" *Gold Cord* (Ft. Washington PA: Literature Crusade, 1991). Used by permission of publisher.

[10] Used by permission of author.

[11] Used by permission of author.

[12] Boston: Beacon Press, 1962/1963.

[13] New York: Harper & Row, 1965.

[14] New York: Avon Books/Macmillan, 1965.

[15] New York: Doubleday, 1989.

[16] New York: Doubleday, 1989.

[17] New York: A. A. Knopf, 1923.

[18] Used by permission of author.

[19] Used by permission of author.

[20] Used by permission of author.

[21] *Prayers* (New York: Seabury Press, 1962/1981) 5.

[22] "For Katrina's Sundial," *The Poems of Henry Van Dyke* (New York: Charles Scribner's Sons, 1911) 341.

[23] Used by permission of author.